CHOOSING A LEGAL STRUCTURE FOR YOUR BUSINESS

Books in the "Run Your Own Business" Series

Choosing a Legal Structure for Your Business

Stuart A. Handmaker

Prentice Hall

Library of Congress Cataloging-in-Publication Data

Handmaker, Stuart A.
   Choosing a legal structure for your business / Stuart A.
Handmaker
       p.   cm.
   ISBN 0-13-603366-0
   1. Business enterprises—Law and legislation—United States—
Popular works.   I. Title.
KF1355.Z9H36   1997
346.73′065—dc21   96-50327
                                                                 CIP

Printed in the United States of America

Printing 10   9   8   7   6   5   4   3   2

ATTENTION: CORPORATIONS AND SCHOOLS

Prentice Hall books are available at quantity discounts with bulk purchase for educational, business, or sales promotional use. For information, please write to Prentice Hall Special Sales, 240 Frisch Court, Paramus, NJ 07652. Please supply: title of book, ISBN number, quantity, how the book will be used, date needed.

PRENTICE HALL
Paramus, NJ 07652

On the World Wide Web at http://www.phdirect.com

ISBN 0-13-603366-0

Contents

5   LLC, The New Kid on the Block   *77*

6   Playing for the Franchise   *89*

7   What Else Do I Need to Know?   *111*

Appendix A, Articles of Incorporation   *131*

Appendix B, Bylaws   *135*

Appendix C, Partnership Agreement   *143*

Appendix D, Certificate of Limited Partnership   *150*

Appendix E, Limited Partnership Agreement   *153*

Index   *166*

Preface

Choosing a Legal Structure for Your Business is a lighthearted, but thorough, exploration of the challenges faced by each of the thousands of Americans each month who decide to cast off the presumed comforts of lifelong employment with a large, impersonal corporate body, and strike off on their own. Often, the lessons they learn about leasing, buying, hiring, selling, insuring, and organizing come at substantial expense, not because of greed or stupidity, but because the entrepreneur was unaware of what to ask, or of whom to ask. Even the scholar who can go straight to the source in discussing the effects of seismic disturbances on poultry production in the Crimea, is confused when asked to sign a personal guarantee on his new corporation's lease on a pizza delivery truck.

The book is written primarily around the fabric of selecting the form of business to use—proprietorship, partnership, corporation or Limited Liability Company, but along the way there is an exploration of virtually all the issues a fledgling business person faces. Directed to investors of all levels of sophistication, the book is written to provide an affordable crash course in the basics of investing in one's self, with suggestions that can prevent some expensive and serious mistakes. The author, attorney Stuart Handmaker, is a graduate of Stanford University and a veteran of over forty years of practicing law, most of which have been in a mid-sized firm in Louisville, Kentucky, where he has represented manufacturers, wholesalers, retailers, and service providers. *Choosing a Legal Structure for Your Business* is a distillation of the questions and answers, the problems and solutions, the pitfalls and triumphs that he and his clients have experienced throughout the latter half of this century.

Introduction

Thanks for dropping in to visit. You've shared with me some very exciting news; you've decided to go into business for yourself, and start lining your own pockets with bucks instead of somebody else's. "How do you think I should put this package together?" you asked.

"That's a bigger question than you might have thought," I said. "Have you got all day to listen?"

"No, I don't," you told me. "Why don't you just write it all out and let me read it when I have the time to sit down and digest it and think about it?"

I did. Here it is.

In *The Revolutionist's Handbook,* George Bernard Shaw said that "He who can, does; he who cannot, teaches." In writing this, I have the earnest hope to offer a modest bit of evidence to discredit Shaw's conclusion. Fortunately, there will be no clear measure of the degree of my success in the endeavor, and, equally fortunately for the situation, if not for Shaw, the fact that Shaw has been dead for nearly a hundred years lessens the likelihood of his arguing the point.

This book, then, is a little effort to teach some very, very basic structural rules. It is a modest discussion designed to point out some murky outlines of shapes that one should be aware of, if he has thoughts of creating a company of his own, and being his own boss. The path to success is not pointed out here, only a few of the major potholes that need to be avoided as you plod down the road.

Before dipping into substance, it's appropriate to set out a few ground rules and a few definitions. First, the ground rules: this entire little book is written from the standpoint of one who has been a member of the bar of the Commonwealth of Kentucky for over forty years. This is not a suggestion that I am entitled to an award for endurance; it is to point out that the suggestions and conclusions which follow are those appropriate to the law of Kentucky, and not necessarily to the law of any other jurisdiction.

Throughout the twentieth century, the strong trend has been toward standardization of the laws of the various states, and the distinctions and differences are minimal, compared to the old days. Fifty years ago, anyone with any degree of sophistication at all always made sure that he did his incorporating in Delaware and his divorcing in Nevada. But then along came the spoilsports of the American Bar, the commission on uniform laws, and statutes began to follow the same pattern as fast food restaurants by being the same wherever you went. Most of the large distinctions, and many of the petty distinctions, between the laws of the various states were obliterated, as the state legislatures started to fall in line, adopting essentially identical statutes. And, at the same time, in another move toward essential uniformity the Courts of the various states began to accept more readily the reasoning and precedent of one another, considering it valid, even though it came from way out there a hundred or more miles away. Our regional and jurisdictional differences were disappearing.

I am certain that there are many who are comforted by sameness and predictability, who look forward with confidence that the next Holiday Inn will be the same as the last one, and who rejoice in the knowledge that there is exactly the same amount of cholesterol in the McDonald's cheeseburger sold in Vancouver as the one sold in Key West. There are also those who have a sense of loss and grief arising from the same facts. But this is not an essay on conformity as the ultimate death of the human spirit; ours here is but to recognize what is. And what is, today, is that the broad acceptance of creations such as the Uniform Partnership Law, the Uniform Business Corporation Law, and similar structures, has almost totally removed the distinctions among the laws of the sister states.

Truth to tell, there is something to the argument that uniformity of laws has a bit more going for it than uniformity of cheeseburgers. Business in America today is no respecter of state boundaries and, even philosophically, there is a stronger reason for a businessman to expect predictability in the enforceability of a contract than in the resilience of a motel mattress. Anyway, the ground rule is that there is still no complete assurance that the rule of law that applies in one state will apply in another. And when it comes to state taxation of business operation (or, indeed, to state taxation of anything), the rules vary all over the place.

Next general rule: be not comforted by knowing that something is usually so, or almost always so, or hardly ever the case. If a business operation is legal in every county in the United States except for a little enclave in eastern Washington, that will be of little solace to those of you operating in Spokane. So, while I am talking in the general, it is highly likely that you are hearing in the particular, and you need to be on guard about that.

One more general rule—perhaps the most important of all: while I have endeavored to offer you here the best of my recollections, and there are no intentional inaccuracies in the pages that follow, I urge you, I beseech you, I pray you (and my insurance company joins fervently in the prayer) that you accept what is said here as but an invitation to seek your own professional confirmation of virtually everything except the page numbers. I urge this because each of us is sometimes in error; because what is true here may not be true there; because what is true now may not be true tomorrow; and because every conclusion is based upon a number of factors which may include some which you meant to consider but didn't.

Now, as to some definitions: I claim the prerogative of Humpty Dumpty in Alice in Wonderland. "When I use a word, it means just what I choose it to mean—neither more nor less." I admit, however, an obligation to a bit more consistency than Humpty Dumpty, but the important factor here is not one of concordance with the spirit of Webster. Rather, it is one of communicating. Accord me, then, please, this favor: in these pages know that when I use these words which I have defined for these purposes, these are the ideas which I am trying to convey. Thereafter, feel free to slam the cover on these pages and return to some other definitions that you like better, but while you and I are having this conversation, an understanding of what I am saying has to be based on what I mean by the words I have used.

When I refer to a *business*, I am discussing any ongoing endeavor or effort directed at generating money for its owners and operators, by the application of thought, energy, effort, and property. It includes manufacturing, distributing, wholesaling, and retailing. It includes services and products and arts and performances. It does not include governmental operations or charities or public schools, but it does include proprietary schools, and private hospitals. It includes neurosurgeons and violinists and pirates and prostitutes. It even includes lawyers. Well, some lawyers.

The word *company* has nothing to do with who is coming to dinner. But it is also not limited to corporations. Its use here, as its use in the law, refers to any kind of business structure—a proprietorship, a partnership, a corporation, or whatever, and it tells you nothing about the type or size of entity. That's also worth remembering when you look at the names of others with whom you are dealing.

The term *person* includes not only the living and breathing human type. It extends to legally created "persons" such as corporations, and trusts, and estates. It is anything which or who can act or spend money or commit a crime, or sue or be sued.

The term *property* refers to that which can be owned. There is real property, which is land and that which is built upon it. There is tangible personal property, which is physical, moveable, touchable, such as automobiles and chairs and books and tangerines and cow pies and television sets and so on. There is intangible personal property such as money and stocks and bonds and patents and franchises. If you can sell it, or if you can steal it, it's property.

Other definitions will be thrown in from time to time, usually with fair warning.

1

You're Going into What?

Hundreds, if not thousands of times a day in these United States, another dream takes the first step toward reality. An individual throws down the gauntlet, takes the bit in her teeth, puts her shoulder to the wheel, fixes her sights firmly on the horizon, plants her feet on the ground, tightens her belt, casts caution to the winds, and goes into business for herself. The American dream is one of infinite success stemming from energy, devotion, purposefulness, steadfastness, courage, and wisdom. Each of us realizes, deep down, that "I am the little engine that could." Each of us knows in his heart of hearts that "I can do it better."

Fortunately for the health of our collective dream, many of those who take the plunge succeed. They learn to balance the competitive pulls of creditors and employees and ambition and family; they learn to balance fantasy against reality. Unlike the song, they seek and find the possible dream.

Dozens of variables enter into a decision of what shape the business structure should assume, and the weight to be given each is not susceptible to measurement. You can, and probably should, read dozens of scholarly works, far more comprehensive than this one. You can research the successes and failures that others have experienced in your chosen field, and probably that is an even greater "should," although it is one much more frequently honored in the breach rather than the observance. Or you can lick your finger, hold it up in the air, close your eyes, and decide which direction the wind is coming from.

The most common approach, of course, is to engage in deep discussion with friends who like to talk a lot and to pontificate on virtually every subject upon which they have little understanding and no experience. These are the experts who have profound knowledge of the real secrets of mankind, such as why you must always (or perhaps never) purchase replacement parts for your car which are recommended by the manufacturer, what the secret ingredient is in my beer that causes it to be so much more enjoyable than yours, and how they paid off and shipped out the guys who invented light bulbs that never burn out and pantyhose that never tear. These conversations begin, commonly, with "I got this friend who started off with absolutely nothing, I mean nothing, you know, and he set up this crypto-dipto partneration, and it had this real weird provision that made Internal Revenue pay him instead of him paying them, you know, and that's what you oughta do."

Well, just in case you don't follow that route, here are a couple of things to think about.

Let's start off with these questions:

1. What is the product or service that I am going to offer to the folks?

2. Where will I get it; i.e., if I'm going to buy it, from whom will I buy it and how and for how much? If I'm going to make it, what do I need to make it with? If I am going to do it, do I have enough training and knowledge to do it well?

3. What is there about the product or the service or the time and place that it is available, or the price and manner of delivery or whatever, that will attract the purchaser to me instead of the other guy?

4. What do I need to start with in terms of capital, and where will I get it? As for the part of my capital that doesn't come out of my own pocket, what do I need to promise to my money source in terms of earnings and repayment?

5. Who do I need to have with me, to work with me, and to deal with me, where will I find them, and, once I've found them, what kind of a deal do I make with them?

6. What will I charge and how will I collect, and what can I reasonably expect as the results of each month's operation over the next three years?

7. What are my threats, my worries, and my fears, and how do I protect against them?

8. Where can I hope, realistically, to be five years from now?

There is only one wrong answer to any of these questions. That's "I don't know." Once having answered the questions, it is essential to bear in mind that the answers can change from time to time, so long as one remembers that each change may carry with it a fairly substantial price tag.

One of the more memorable stories that I have heard was related in a television interview of the president of the Sony Corporation. What he said, in essence, was that after his company had received a fairly large black eye for backing Beta as the videotape road to follow, when the rest of the world apparently had opted for VHS, he felt the need to open some new doors for Sony in the area of consumer electronics. So he took off for the United States, the home of his greatest concentration of customers, to find out what they wanted Sony to do. Rather than hiring a market research organization to perform for him the most central of all corporate functions, he chose to do the job himself.

For a period of time which was described as three weeks, but which I suspect to have been considerably less, he walked the streets of major American cities, and visited with the people in their places of business, places of entertainment, and homes. He was not asking questions, he was observing, and asking himself one question: "What is it that these people really would like to have, but probably don't know that they would like to have?"

By the time he returned home, he had the answer. Sony produced the Walkman, and enjoyed a huge well deserved success for doing so. Whether society in general is improved by the existence of millions of little plastic boxes stuck in persons' pockets or their ears, and whether the quality of what they are hearing is beneficial to them in any way is not the question before the house, what the product did for Sony is. And the lesson the corporate president was teaching is clear; he found the product.

The touch isn't limited to the manufacturer. To the joy of his shareholders and relatives and the dismay of small town shopkeepers in a thousand friendly little towns, Sam Walton found his key in the monster-mega-huge-discount one-stop homogenized store set out in the middle of a field near the small town. And the ultimate (or, at least, so far, the ultimate) revision of our concept of "store" was rewritten.

And now retailing has taken the next step, obviating the need for parking facilities at all. Shop via catalog or in response to the television huckster, and order by telephone, charging it to your credit card. All of these operations represent new systems devised over a short period of time, by development from idea to concept to manifestation to saturation to blight. The important factor here is just one: somebody or bodies did the creating and waxed even wealthier than the lottery could make them. Luck? Probably not.

Others have conquered the world, not with new products or new systems of distribution, but with new and different forms of services offered. There are still those among us who remember the day when, if your hair began to stick out over your ears, you went to a barber and paid him fifty cents, instead of going to a hair stylist for fifty dollars. Yet, many "hair stylists" succeed, and they do so because they are offering the public what a sufficiently broad segment of the public wants and is willing to pay for.

Time was when the thought of competing with the United States Postal Service would have been on a level with the thought of starting your own Marine Corps. And those were days when a letter was delivered for three cents. To the proper addressee. Before a month went by. Yet, today, even though we are, more than ever before, communicating electronically by phone and fax and modem, we have seen huge success stories in courier services, ranging from Federal Express and UPS to Uncle Joe's Handy Dandy Neighborhood Courier Delivery. And they work. And, to some extent at least, many of them would work successfully even if the Postal Service had not jettisoned its competence back around 1970 or so.

Of course, most of the success stories of any generation are not based upon the invention of a fantastic new product, or the development of an entirely new distribution system, or the creation of a brand new type of service to offer. Far more frequently, the business grew from a perceived need based on location (the nearest pizza parlor is ten miles away), or on reputation (people come here to see *me* not because of the name on the sign), or on a modest change of purpose (all they want to do here is handle real estate sales, and I could succeed with a rental agency), or something of that sort. That, perhaps, is as it should be, and perhaps as it will be with you. So let's look at some of the available forms your business can take.

John Doe, Prop.

The oldest, the simplest, and the most prevalent form of business structure is the simple one-person proprietorship. I take my saved up money, and I rent a location. I buy and install whatever equipment and fixtures I need, and I receive my licenses. I open my doors every morning, and I close my doors every night. Because my customers pay me two dollars for what cost me one dollar, I make a living.

There is a certain splendor in having no limitations at all on what you spend your money on. As an individual proprietor, whatever is in the till, or in the business account, is your money. It is yours to spend on enlarging the store, or redecorating the store, or buying new merchandise, or opening a branch. It is also yours to spend on a seven-day cruise in the Caribbean, or a new Ferrari, or a six-foot television dish receiver that brings in the soccer games from Australia. And you don't have to pay yourself a salary or a bonus or a commission or a dividend to have the money to spend. Just reach in the till, grab a handful, and blow it.

The reason for suggesting a spending spree at this stage of the lecture, before you have even opened up for business, is to make a specific point. If it's solely your business, it's solely your money, and no one, absolutely no one, can interfere, not even the Internal Revenue Service. (Does it ever bother you that Internal Revenue is referred to as a "service"? Somehow, I don't feel served by them. Nothing else that brings disaster down on me calls itself a service. "Hello, this is your chronic heart disease service calling." "Sorry I'm late; I just had an arm broken and my head bashed in by our friendly neighborhood mugging service.")

Anyway, back to the question at hand. There is a normal route that we pursue when we confuse related concepts. One concept is that of which expenditures I can subtract from what I receive as income in order to determine the sum of taxable income that I pay a percentage of, as tax. A very different (but related) concept is what I have a right to spend my money on. The folks at Internal Revenue can tell me (and they do) that when I'm computing my taxes, I have no right at all to deduct from income the amount that I spend traveling to Las Vegas for the weekend. But Internal Revenue does not have, and never has had, and, Lord willing and the creek don't rise, never will have, the right to tell me when and whether I can spend money on my own chosen damn foolishness. What I'm entitled to do, and what I'm entitled to deduct in calculating my taxes are two different things.

So, the simple rule of entrepreneurship is to open my own business, take in lots more than I spend, set a bit aside for a rainy day in the store, and all the rest is mine to do with as I see fit.

Nothing could be easier. Right? But, in some situations, it is also true that nothing could be scarier. Please take careful note of the operative words in the previous sentence. They are: "IN SOME SITUATIONS."

The beauty of the proprietorship is its simplicity; the terror of the proprietorship, on the other hand, is its simplicity. That's because there's only one you. The you who opens up the shop in the morning and takes care of customers and receives the money is the same you who goes home at night and owns a lovingly restored MGB roadster. So what? Here's what.

If you fail to pay the rent on the store, or if you have refused to pay for some supplies delivered to you because you feel they aren't what you ordered, or if a customer slipped and fell in the doorway to the store on something that somebody else dropped there, you may very likely find yourself on the receiving end of a lawsuit. If you do, the suit's not just against the store, it's against you.

Someone has coined a statistic to the effect that of all the lawsuits that go to trial, something very close to fifty percent of the persons involved end up disappointed. The saddest part of the statistic is that the guy who ends up disappointed could be you. And when the bad guy has a judgment against you which you haven't paid, his henchman, the sheriff, comes around to pick up your very own property, and to sell it to pay off the judgment. Maybe he picks up the inventory in the store, but when the judgment is against you, you the individual, you the proprietor, the sheriff can just as easily take that lovingly restored MGB. Or your fishing equipment. Or the diamond lavaliere your great-grandmother left you. It's all hanging out there; it's all up for grabs.

Of course, you can and should protect yourself with insurance against most risks. Certainly, you can be and should be and will be insured against the claim of the customer who falls in your doorway, or the customer who eats your pies and gets food poisoning, or the customer whose fur coat was destroyed in the fire when your shop burned.

There is, however, one major risk which you cannot insure against, and that, sad to say, is the most likely risk to come to pass. That's the risk of going broke. As will be pointed out later, there is some of that risk which cannot be avoided no matter what type of business structure you establish, but the risk is clearly the greatest when it's you and you alone running the show.

Other negatives to the proprietorship stem from the same considerations, although they are not necessarily limited to the legal aspects of the structure.

Presumably, you seek the degree of success which will permit you to be away from the business some of the time—for lunch, for the afternoon, for a two-day bout with the flu, even for a several-week vacation to enjoy some of that which you have worked so hard to accumulate. You will have employees of some sort, therefore, and some of them will have the loyalty and the smarts to watch the store while you're gone. But they are, and will remain, employees, and their devotion to your success, no matter how deep, will probably not be the same as yours. It if were, they'd be your competitors instead of your employees.

A chronic disease of the entrepreneur is the inability to delegate. Nobody can do anything as well as I can, and that's why I'm here. I can't stand the thought of somebody else making decisions which affect my well being. She does all right as long as I'm watching, but I'm afraid to turn my back. Sure, he's been with me for twenty-five years; that's because I tell him what to do.

The result of this self-annointed corner on decision making is the limitation on growth that it imposes. If the only person who can make the proper decision is me, then the outer wall of my room is the limit of my horizon.

Understand that these limitations are not necessarily turn offs to the proprietorship. If I can handle the initial investment and the costs of an ongoing operation without subjecting that restored MGB to an unreasonable risk, and if I can earn sufficient income to take care of my needs in a one-man operation, there is nothing in the constitution requiring me to extend myself and to take chances and to employ strangers and to wake up in the middle of the night with a headache and a pulse rate of 150 because I suddenly couldn't remember whether the dingbat I hired to run the suburban branch was smart enough to turn off the gas when he locked the shop up for the weekend. I can always find and hire able and loyal employees, if I am sufficiently selective and sufficiently generous; or I can limit the operation to what I can comfortably do alone.

Further, of course, there are some endeavors that are more appropriately run as individual proprietorships, by nature of the undertaking. The sculptor or painter who has a studio, creates his works, and sells them, the composer of chamber music, the reader of tarot cards, or the birthday-party magician, require little capital investment and run minimal risk of liability. The shoe repair man, the piano teacher, and the chimney sweep, also, fit the pattern of the individual entrepreneur.

This, of course, is not to say that the same business form couldn't be just as applicable in the case of the person who owns and operates a tavern, or a fishing boat, or a frame shop. And, of course, it applies to dentists, brain surgeons, and lawyers. And counterfeiters, embezzlers, and cat burglars.

So, having decided to cast your lot with the great and exciting capitalistic world, and having found satisfying answers to the eight questions on pages 8–9, you're off to the races. What do you do?

Well, in no particular order, you need to:

1. Nail down relationships with your lawyer, your accountant, and your banker. This is not to say that you can't handle these things yourself, without outside professional counsel; you can also take out your own appendix with a soup spoon, but be sure you sharpen the spoon enough before you make the incision.

2. Decide on the name under which you will operate, and do whatever is necessary to determine if it is available and, if so, register it. This very important step is often overlooked, with a result that you spend a bundle establishing and creating a value in a fanciful and valuable business name which you don't own and cannot protect. As a general rule, you don't need to formally register your own given name and surname, but even there, some care is recommended. If your name is Charlie HaagenDaas, get some advice before you open your ice cream store.

3. Find out what you need by way of licensing for your chosen type of business and your location. Some, but not most, businesses need special licenses no matter where they will be. To sell alcoholic beverages of any sort, for example, both the person and the location need governmental approvals. In most cities in Kentucky for any business you need an occupational license tax permit. The fee for this is quite modest, but it registers you to pay your occupational license tax each year, of some 2% (more or less, depending on the city or county) of your income. Remember, however, that to pay 2% of your income to the city is not an income tax. Cities are constitutionally prohibited from charging income tax. So they don't. They charge you an occupational license tax, and it's just that the way they figure out how much you owe them for the privilege of engaging in business is to base it on your income, but it's not an income tax. That's quite clear, isn't it? How could you have ever thought otherwise?

4. Secure your registration numbers from the Internal Revenue Service and the State. The Internal Revenue Service issues you something called an EIN (for Employer Identification Number) which is like your business's own social security number. It's the number which will appear on your employer's withholding tax return, and your business income tax returns, and it is so vital that the bank won't let you open up a business account without it. The State will be happy to give you a registration number, which serves for income taxes which you'll withhold from employees, and for your sales tax reporting too, as well as for various other little uses.

5. Determine the location from which you will operate, and, assuming that you don't own it, negotiate and enter into a lease with the owner. For the lease, you need to consider the length of the lease, the options to renew, if any, the rental to pay, the permitted uses of the property, who pays what (i.e., are taxes, insurance and repairs the obligations of the landlord or the tenant?), and a number of other customary subjects of most leases, such as rights to alter the building, rights of access, and the like.

You need, of course, to be sure that the location is zoned for your business. Every location in most major cities is the subject of zoning of some sort or other, and the zoning classification describes what type of business may be conducted there. And recognize that zoning is not just a matter of whether the operation is innocuous or not. There are classifications where it is permissible to have a junk yard, a cattle slaughtering operation, or a steel foundry, but not a flower shop.

6. Take a copy of your business plan to your bank (whattya mean, what business plan? It's the answers to the eight magic questions on pages 8–9 that you already dealt with, plus an extended discussion of how you're going to take care of everything, and all) and set out for your banker how much you'll need from his bank at each step along the way, and how clear is your ability to pay the bank off at the drop of a hat at any time.

7. Design, purchase, and install fixtures, supplies, and, if appropriate, inventory.

8. Be sure that you have cash on hand to handle normal operating expenses for at least two months (and, preferably, three), even if you don't take in the first penny from operations.

9. Enter into contracts with your suppliers, your employees, your service providers (telephone, trash removal, delivery services, etc.). Remember, when we say "contract" we are not limiting ourselves to those twenty-page documents with whereas and now therefore and stuff. You've entered into a contract when you smile, say, "I'll pay you five bucks an hour, and you'll start tomorrow morning, and no, there ain't no fringes," and she says, "OK, I'll see ya."

10. Say some prayers, take a deep breath, kiss your spouse goodbye, stop shaking, and have at it.

3

I'd Like You to Meet My Partner

THE BASICS

Probably, the first form of business structure to develop beyond the one-person proprietorship was that of the simple two-person partnership. Smith and Jones each kicked in two hundred pounds and bought the village pub. They worked together, side by side, serving ale and (one hopes) washing the tankards. At the end of the week, whatever shillings there were left in the cash box were divided equally between them, and so they prospered.

In another scenario, Old Man Mercer (those were the days when anyone over the age of 40 was "Old Man") had a more than attractive dry goods store and a less than attractive spinster daughter. So, when young Philip Philander asked for the maiden's hand, his chivalry was rewarded with a half-interest in the dry goods store.

Those were the simpler days. Partnerships were created to be cooperative ventures, not tax plans. The common law rules of partnerships were developed in the courts of England and, later, in American courts as well. Stated as a slight oversimplification, the rules were these: any partner could enter into an agreement, binding the partnership and *binding the partners.* Any person could deal with any of the partners, and he could rely on the promise of that one partner as being equal to the joint promises of all the partners, just as if he were dealing with all of the partners simultaneously.

Each partner had an equal right with each other partner to anything and everything. On the death or insanity of any partner, the partnership was automatically dissolved. On dissolution, the assets of the partnership were applied to the debts of the firm, and if there weren't enough assets, the creditors could go after the assets of any or all of the partners. Any assets left over were divided equally among the partners.

The system was good, clean, and, above all, predictable. And it is the predictability which matters the most. There are those who believe that one of the primary virtues of the Anglo-American system of jurisprudence is the enshrinement of predictability. If I know what the rules are today, and if I can be certain that the rules will be the same tomorrow, then I can make my decisions based on those rules and live with the consequences. There are no good rules or bad rules; there is no fair or unfair. So long as I know that C will always follow B, and B will always follow A, and so long as I have the right to choose A or not A, I have no right to complain upon finding that I'm stuck with C when I chose A.

The rule that any partner could bind the entire partnership did not, however, give any partner total license to do whatever he saw fit. That rule governed the rights of an outsider who did business with the partnership by dealing with one partner, but it did not govern the rights of the partners against one another. This was because the partners could enter into any form of contractual relationship they chose to control their rights as between or among themselves. They couldn't change the basic laws that control the rights and relationships between the partnership on the one hand and the rest of the world on the other hand, but they could do whatever they liked as amongst themselves.

For example, partner A can enter into a contract with American Wuggle Company to buy a thousand wuggles for the partnership at a price of fifty dollars each, all to be red with blue stripes and all to be delivered Tuesday morning. And the partnership is struck with the deal. No matter that the firm already has a two-year supply of wuggles. No matter that wuggles are available in any color, right here in River City, for thirty-five dollars each. The partnership is stuck with the deal, and Partner B cannot argue that he and Partner C had specifically told A to buy no more wuggles. A is a partner; A entered into an agreement on behalf of the partnership; and the partnership is bound. And if the partnership can't pay for them, American Wuggle can come after the assets of the partnership, and the assets of Partner A and (horror of horrors) the personal assets of Partner B and Partner C as well. Even C's lovingly restored MGB. That's partnerships for you.

But there's a brighter side, and that lies in the right of the partners to spell out in specific and clear terms the relationships of the partners. For example, in the case of the wuggles, A, B, and C could have a provision in their partnership agreement to the effect that no partner can obligate the partnership on any contract which will call for spending over $500.00 without the consent of at least one other partner.

Now this kind of provision would have no effect upon the question of whether the partnership was or was not liable for the purchase of all one thousand of those red-and-blue wuggles. They're stuck. After all, American Wuggle Co. had no way to know what was in the partnership agreement of A, B, and C. But B and C know. And B and C are sore. They are more than miffed; they are livid. And the partnership agreement gives them the right to stick A right in the gotchas. A violated the partnership agreement, and B and C can require A personally to pay for and take all those wuggles himself, or to repay the partnership for whatever it loses on the deal. This works out fine so long as A has the means to pay for his error. If not, it's the partnership and the other partners who are stuck.

The main beauty of the system, of course, lies not in the fact that A will end up with his basement and garage filled to the rafters with red-and-blue wuggles. Because of knowledge of the restrictions upon him, he will very probably not enter into such deals, even if his son-in-law is the sales manager for American Wuggle.

So the moral of this extended sermon is a very simple one: if you have the urge to enter into a partnership with anybody, let there be a partnership agreement spelling out very carefully who gets what, who gives what, who does what, and so on. Even then, however, remember that the risk of loss which exceeds the wherewithal of the partnership and the capable partner falls on the other partners.

As the world of business organizations became more complicated, most states developed bodies of statutory law relating to partnerships, in the same way (sorta) that states developed statutes of intestate succession. In other words, you could do whatever you wished with your property by way of disposing of it by will (well, almost whatever you wished), but if for any reason you were to die without a will, the state law of intestate (i.e., no will) succession wrote a will for you, and set out in detail how your property passed. In the same way, state partnership statutes provided, in essence, that partners could enter into agreements specifying in detail their roles and their rights in the partnership, but if they didn't have an agreement spelling it out, or if they had an agreement which was silent on one specific point or another, the statutory rules would constitute their agreement.

As we noted above in other contexts, the next developmental step was the passage of the Uniform Partnership Act by virtually every state, and the codification of these rules. We need to recognize that even where the states adopt a "Uniform" law, it's not always totally uniform. Various states may omit a section or alter a section, or exercise the full range of legislative integrity by making a special exemption for somebody's generous brother-in-law, or whatever. You know how it is with legislatures these days. It's filthy thankless work but somebody hasta do it. Anyway, the Uniform Partnership Act, or the UPA as it is fondly known, primarily does this: it spells out and "codifies" (or expresses somewhat directly and clearly) the rights and liabilities and expectations of those persons dealing with partnerships, and of partnerships in dealing with others; it places some limitations upon the scope of partnership agreements than may be entered into; and it provides the rules of the game as among partners whose agreements have failed to specify.

So that's what partnerships are; why would you want to enter into one anyway? There are personal reasons, and business reasons, and tax reasons.

Charlie and I are both dentists, and we've been good friends for a long time and we trust each other. If we are partners we can save a lot of money on the equipment that we need and can share, we can economize on support staff and rent and telephone, and we can look after each other's patients when one of us is away on vacation or at a seminar or whatever. Besides, some collegiality not only makes practice more fun, it also gives me a sounding board to test out my professional decision-making process. Or ...

Marianne and I can each afford to be out of the home about half of the time, but not full time, and we think having a little shop would be a great idea and give each of us a sense of independence, but fixing it up and stocking it will take more than either of us can come up with alone. Or ...

I am a world-class mustard maker. I can prepare anything from the simplest to the most complex, from the sweetest to the bitterest. But I couldn't sell a penny glass of iced tea to a man dying of thirst. Bob, on the other hand, can sell anything to anybody at any time for any price, but he couldn't make anything. If the two of us put our talents together, we'll enjoy huge success in a month; alone, either of us would starve.

These are the cases that call for the simple *general partnership*. They are really not that different from the proprietorship that we were discussing a while ago, except that there are two of us with competing (even if we agree with each other usually) interests, with disparate personalities and emotions, and distinct non-business involvements. There exists, therefore, a clear need to spell out the rights and obligations of the partners vis-a-vis one another.

At this point, there is another one of those vignettes from the real world that I can't help throwing in here. (Actually, I *can* help it; I have a perfectly functional "delete" key on my computer. It's that I *choose* to tell you the story.)

On dozens, if not hundreds, of occasions I have started a meeting with two, three, or four persons who have come together to begin a business together; usually, a group of physicians, but sometimes those of a more noble calling. They tell me (after some jockeying for position as to who is the spokesman of the group) that they would like to form a partnership so they can practice together. Then the spokesman says, "But we don't need one of those long and complicated partners' agreement things because we all know each other and we trust each other." At this point, I usually take them into our library and point out a large set of books bound in light tan cloth, with a red strip and a black strip across the spine.

"See those books," I tell them. "Those books are all written opinions of Courts, and all expressing the rules of partnership law. You know where the Courts got those cases to write about? Every one of them arose when one partner sued another. And you know something else? Every one of those partnerships started off with a bunch of folks who trusted each other, or they never would have become partners."

The part I didn't need to tell them was that in every one of those cases, the costs of litigation were many times what a definitive partnership agreement would have cost. Which is not to say, of course, that a well drafted partnership agreement is an absolute shield against subsequent problems. Nor is fire insurance an absolute shield against your house burning down. It's just better to have it before the event instead of after.

FORMING THE PARTNERSHIP

Well, as I was saying before the interruption, it would be a good thing to consider what questions a simple general partnership agreement might treat with, so that you and your partner can discuss these questions before they arise. Here are a few:

1. What do we call the partnership?

2. What business will the partnership engage in? Here, there is strong support for being restrictive. "We are going to sell wrenches and pliers from a kiosk in the mall." If we later decide to broaden the scope of our operation, we can amend the agreement.

3. Who are the partners, and what is each one contributing to the partnership? Primarily, here we are talking about money and property as being "contributed" but there are also expertise, reputation, design, and much else that a partner can "contribute." Remember, though, that once contributed, something belongs to the partnership, not to the individual partner. I can contribute the results of my creative genius, but not my brilliance itself.

For this discussion, the terms "capital" and "net worth" are the same. They refer to the net value of what the owner of a Company owns. If my business has total assets of a value of $5,000, consisting of $1,000 in cash, and $1,000 in accounts receivable, and $3,000 in inventory, but I still owe the factory $1,500 for the inventory, my capital is $3,500, i.e., the $5,000 in assets, less what anybody else (here, the factory) has a superior claim for, i.e., the $1,500 that I'm going to have to send to the factory. So, my "capital" or "net worth" is $3,500. If I'm part of a partnership, however, that $3,500 is the net worth of the whole partnership. If I put in half of the money we started with, and Sam put in the other half, then my "capital" is now $1,750 (i.e., 50% of $3,500), and Sam's capital is $1,750 (the other 50%). Unless, of course, we have something different in our partnership agreement.

Remember further, in this regard, that there is no reason to assume that everyone who joins the partnership will contribute the same amount of capital, or will have the same percentage of ownership, or even that the proportions of ownership will mirror the ratio of the contributions. Maybe Garfunkel needs Simon badly enough that Simon gets 60% of the partnership for only 35% of the total contributed capital.

4. How will the profits and the losses be distributed among the partners? There is no need for uniformity here. Losses can be in one ratio up to a stated amount and in another ratio thereafter, while profits are divided in another system altogether. Similarly, while in the simplest case, the ratio of profit-sharing will be the same as the ratio of ownership (i.e., A puts in two-thirds of the capital and gets two-thirds of the profit, while B, for the other one-third of the capital, gets one-third of the profits), there is no compelling reason that this must be the case.

Profits and losses, also, can be determined in any number of ways other than ratios, ranging from 50-50 to straight commission to percentages of the weekly take, to part one way and part the other.

This area, the manner of sharing profits and losses, has all kinds of ramifications. It offers a whole selection of opportunities and options, depending on why we are forming a partnership in the first place. Let's look at several scenarios.

Agitate and Litigate, two young lawyers, filled with ambition, form a partnership to practice law. Agitate is from a poor but honest family. His parents are struggling neurosurgeons who can hardly feed themselves and pay the mortgage on their tar paper shack adjoining the scrap yard. Agitate worked his way through school and has monstrous student loan payments to meet.

Litigate, on the other hand, is the only son of J. Prufrock Litigate, a prominent shipping clerk at Wal-Mart, who has seniority, a funded retirement program, and virtually limitless cash to give to his son. So Litigate contributes $25,000 to the firm to buy its library and furniture, and to fund its initial operations. Agitate, on the other hand, contributes only a tattered copy of *Black's Law Dictionary*, which is all that he owns. Yet both young lawyers will—and do—give the firm their full and complete energy and effort, attracting business, winning cases, and earning fees. How should their formula for dividing profits be affected by the fact that Litigate provided virtually all the capital contribution and all the beginning assets? Probably, not at all.

Here, Litigate deserves to earn a reasonable return on the money he invested and put at risk. But the money rolling in the door has been earned by the talent and effort of the two young lawyers, not by the magnificence of office decor and the handsome bindings on the library books. So we generously agree to pay to Litigate an amount which would be a reasonable return on his $25,000 investment—perhaps $2,000 a year—and split everything else equally.

Compare that situation to another law firm, Obfuscate and Cogitate. Harrumph P. Obfuscate has been practicing law for thirty years in our city and has earned a huge sack of bucks, confusing and befuddling courts, opponents, and government agencies. He has a handsome office, all the assets of which he has depreciated at least once, fully, but which are serviceable and impressive. Obfuscate has an enviable client list, and is eagerly sought out by the executive officers of many of the largest local companies. Cogitate, on the other hand, is eager, bright, penniless, and hardworking, but something of a nerd. He is a true scholar, and can provide Obfuscate with just the research and documents that are needed. He may be a diamond in the rough, but there is so much slag around the stone that more than one grinding machine will be burned out before the facets begin to sparkle. Still, Obfuscate wishes to offer Cogitate a partnership.

In this case, much of the firm's success over the first few years will derive from the existing entity—Obfuscate's handsome offices, his more handsome client list, and the patina of success and competence and solidity that his presence brings to the scene. Yet, truth be known, the fees that come through the door are earned by the research and writing and document drafting that Cogitate's sixteen-hour days produce, while Obfuscate's primary use of his desk is to keep the liter of Maker's Mark in the lower left-hand drawer.

So here, our formula is a different one. The firm may (but need not) elect to pay a salary to one of the partners—before the pie-splitting proportions come in to play. Or perhaps we can say that the largest percentage of the first X dollars of income goes to Cogitate, and thereafter the lion's share goes to Obfuscate. Or perhaps Obfuscate gets 90% and Cogitate gets 10% the first year, and there is a guaranteed percentage increase each year to Cogitate—or maybe a guaranteed increase if the firm earns XX dollars. Maybe the formula provides for eventual equality; probably, in a law firm, it does not. In a medical practice, on the other hand, the normal practice is to provide for a rapid movement toward equality in many cases (depending on the field of specialty, the degree to which the specialty and the practice are lucrative, and on numerous other criteria).

The two contrasting cases just presented have these similarities: (a) We recognize that there are some elements of operation which can be compensated in a manner different from, or additional to a share of the earnings, such as by salary, or commission, or bonus, or interest for the use of money, or, perhaps, by a royalty for use of a patent or an idea, or another similar means; and (b) the ratio of sharing the residual profits can be based on contributed capital, or contributed effort, or relative availability in the market place of whatever it is that a party brings to the mix (such as control of a choice business location, or an exclusive contractual right for a product of central importance, or whatever).

These, however, have been professional practices where the product being sold is personal service. What about the business where a tangible product is being offered? Let's assume that Baskin has his plate full—he operates successful tire and muffler repair shops all over Indiana, and has built a fine name and a visible identity which attracts customers from all over. He also has money to invest, but he certainly doesn't want to work any harder than he is now working. Along comes Robbins, who is trained and knowledgeable in repairing tires and mufflers and in running shops, but Robbins can't afford the price of his own shop, and Robbins's credit isn't enough to swing a deal.

So a partnership is formed between Mr. Baskin and Mr. Robbins to open tire and muffler shops in Kentucky and spread the reputation which Baskin has already built.

Baskin will put up 90% of the money to open the first Kentucky store, in Owensboro, and Robbins will squeeze out the other 10%. Robbins will do all the work and Baskin will supply whatever extra money is needed to build the business. But Robbins doesn't want to think of himself as an "employee" even of his own partnership. "Stuff the salary bit," he says. "I'll take my chances, so I can get a bigger piece of the action, because I know I'll succeed and I want my share."

So here we devise a system which is probably on a sliding scale. The first $100,000 (or whatever sum) of earnings is split so as to place a value on Robbins's time devoted to the business, and on Baskin's investment of money and reputation and buying arrangements and whatever. The next $100,000 or so may be split very differently, on the assumption that if the store earns more than $100,000, it must be because of the extraordinary efforts that Robbins is devoting. And maybe profits beyond that point are divided on another concept. So you could end up with something like this:

Profits	Baskin's Share	Robbins's Share
0 -$100,000	60%	40%
$100,000 -$200,000	20%	80%
$200,000 -$300,000	40%	60%
over $300,000	50%	50%

Thus, if the operation earns $80,000 in a year, the split is $48,000–$32,000; if it earns $180,000, the split is $76,000–$104,000; if it earns $280,000, the split is $112,000–$168,000.

These formulas can, of course, be changed from time to time if the parties wish. But it is important to note that where any negotiation ends up depends in large measure on where it started, and changes acceptable to all parties will seldom be of huge proportion.

Let's look at another different type of partnership. Grandpa is sixty years old, and embarrassingly overendowed with wealth; Dad is thirty-five and is making good strides but hasn't built much net worth yet. Kid is two years old, and, so far, has very little wealth, expertise, or reputation. They form G, D & K, a partnership to own and rent real estate. The main idea is to deplete—or at least to avoid further growth in—

Grandpa's holdings, and, maybe, to build up Kid's property interests to help pay for his education.

Grandpa puts up $30,000 cash, making a gift of $10,000 to Dad and $10,000 to Kid, and the three have equal interests in the partnership. The partnership buys an apartment house for $500,000, and gets a mortgage for $470,000, mostly because the bank knows Grandpa and will gladly lend money wherever he signs the note. Dad does the work, fixing up the building, renting it to tenants, making repairs, and the like. Kid's only job is to pose for the ad photos. The three partners split the income equally. Kid's share of the income comes in at his negligible tax bracket, and is put away for his education when he gets older. It's a good deal for Kid, but Grandpa and Dad get a kick out of it, so it's okay.

So let's go back to the list of questions we needed to answer to build the partnership.

5. How will the partners receive money from the firm on a weekly or monthly or whatever basis? Presumably, a partner's drawings will be based to some extent on his calculated share of distributable profit, because there has to be a day of reckoning, and it's more than just bad form to keep on taking out more than one earns. Still, it's not unusual to establish a set weekly, semi-monthly, or monthly draw in dollars, and adjust it periodically against earnings.

6. What will the partners' capital accounts be, and how will they change over time? Your capital account is your share of the ownership of the whole partnership, and is primarily significant in determining who gets what when the partnership breaks up or when you are bought out. That is, if C's capital account is 60% of the aggregate total of all the capital accounts, and if the partnership agreement provides that on dissolution, the assets will be divided among the partners according to the ratio that their capital accounts bear one to the other; then on split-up, C will get 60% of whatever is left.

The essential rule (unless the agreement has some other provision) is that a partner's capital, at any point in time, is equal to his original capital contribution, plus (or minus) his allocated share of net profits (or losses), less his total drawings. So each year, for each partner, you take his beginning capital, add to it his share of the profits, deduct from that whatever he took out of the firm as drawings for the year, and what's left is his new capital account. The total of all partners' capital accounts, remember, is equal to the net worth of the partnership.

7. How are decisions made in the partnership? Do all partners have equal voting power, or are some more powerful than others? Do voting rights change as relative ownership rights change? On what matters does the majority rule (whatever we have decided that an operative majority is) and what matters take 75%, or 80%, or even 100%?

8. Can new partners be added and, if so, how? Can a partner pull out of the partnership? If there is no provision in the agreement with respect to this, the only way that a person can resign from the partnership is to terminate the partnership. If the partnership has more than two members, you will want to have some other arrangement, both for the benefit of the withdrawing partner, so that he can get paid out, and also for the benefit of the remaining partners who don't want to see their Company destroyed just because one of the guys changed his mind.

9. When, and in what events, will the partnership come to an end? Later on, we can discuss alternative provisions to make for this situation, because this is one of the more difficult problems to face when organizing a partnership. Corollary to this discussion is the discussion of what happens when a partner dies.

10. What is to be provided in the partnership agreement with respect to basic housekeeping questions? To some extent, this is a philosophical inquiry, since these matters, like keeping the books, are going to be attended to whether the agreement spells it out or not. The question in each case is, "Do we want to put it in the basic constitutional document, the partnership agreement?" In common parlance, "Do we want it engraved in stone?"

11. What does it take to amend the partnership agreement? If there are only two equal partners, of course, this is an easy question to answer. It would be hard to get a simple majority without having unanimous agreement. But what if there are three? Should two of the three be able to amend the agreement and thus change some very basic expectations that number three had when he entered into this very important understanding? No? Well, what if there are 500 partners? Should one of them have the right to hold up the works for the whole group just to be a dissident?

12. What other provisions, if any, does the group want as a part of the basic compact that glues them together?

One possible solution appears in the sample partnership agreement attached as Appendix C at page 143.

ENDING THE PARTNERSHIP

Now, as I mentioned earlier, in each of these cases, the UPA (that's the Uniform Partnership Act, remember?)

makes a provision to answer the question if the partners failed to do so. For example, under the UPA, any partner can end the partnership at any time, just by saying, "I want out." Death of any partner automatically terminates the firm. So does being adjudicated insane. Under the UPA, there can be no amendment to the partnership agreement without unanimous consent of all partners.

Fortunately (or, maybe, not so fortunately) if a partnership is a success, the whole grows quickly to be greater than the sum of its parts. The Company acquires an identity of its own whose value exists only so long as the entity exists. When Ben agreed with Jerry to make ice cream, something happened, and it wasn't very long until there was a value there which far exceeded the potential value of Ben's Ice Cream + Jerry's Ice Cream. It's a lot easier for Black to sell his cordless drill when he has Decker working with him. And so on.

So who owns this "going concern value"? When it's a partnership, the answer is easy. The partnership does. And all the partners own the partnership.

If that's the case, what happens in the event the partnership comes to an end? Under the UPA, you sell this value if you can; it evaporates if you cannot. Under a well written partnership agreement, however, there are sensible provisions to treat this situation, and they are for everybody's benefit.

Let's look, then, at some of the possible courses of action available to a partnership and to the partners to ease the pain in the event of withdrawal or termination.

First, how about the voluntary termination of the whole partnership? It seems fair in most cases (and note well, please, that "in most cases" does NOT mean "in all cases") to provide that when a majority in number of the partners and a majority in percentage shares of ownership want to end the partnership, the partnership should be ended. The ending of the partnership, however, does not usually mean the end of the business, unless the partnership is ending by reason of the failure of the business. The questions that need to be answered, and the contractual terms that need to be agreed upon from the beginning are ones of their relative rights of the partners. If everyone is in agreement that the business should be sold to an outsider, then the questions are easily answered, the sale is completed, and the proceeds are divided among the various interest units in accordance with their proportionate rights, usually their capital accounts.

In many cases, however, it is well to provide for the first choice of purchasing the business to reside within the partnership group itself. After all, they know it best, they appreciate its value, they can do the most with it, and, therefore, they are the ones willing to pay the most. The recommended provision, therefore, is an arrangement under which one or more partners have a right of first refusal (in other words, the right to match and pay the best offer than can be received from an outsider), or, alternatively, a way of determining the price to be paid and a specified period of time within which a partner has the right to say "I'll take it."

Occasionally, a partnership is composed of a collection of individuals and assets such that there is a specific emotional or professional or intellectual attachment that one of them has to a Company asset. A patent might be most valuable to the partner who invented the process. A business name might be most valuable to the person whose name it is. And so on. Suffice it for here and now to note that it is well within the scope of what's normal to make specific provisions for such situations.

We've mentioned that it might be a good idea to have a provision to let a partner out (assuming that there are three or more) and we've set up a system to pay him out, perhaps over a period of time, and that's fine too. But what happens if our dissenting fellow is a hog who wants to take a ripoff of the firm's product, go into business for himself across the street, and let the rest of us starve? A provision which can take care of that possibility is the covenant against competition, a contractual agreement that one who leaves the firm cannot compete with the firm or steal the partnership's business. The range that such provisions can cover, and the rules of enforceability of such agreements, are the subject of a lengthy discussion which doesn't belong here, but we need to note that such things are possible.

Along with the question of what happens when a partner decides that he would like to leave, there is the other side of that coin. What happens when all of the other partners decide that one of their number has to go? In other words, is there any difference in treatment between the one who leaves because he chooses to and the one who is booted out? In some agreements, there is a difference, but many suggest that it is unwise to draw this distinction. If there is a distinction in the agreement so that one who is kicked out gets all his property rights, but one who leaves of his own volition takes nothing with him, it is in the interest of the remaining partners that the departing partner walks out instead of being thrown out. To bring this about, the remaining partners usually can, if they wish, make the departing partner so miserable that he leaves voluntarily, and those are rather unhappy days for all.

The death of a partner is something which should be thoughtfully treated in a well written partnership agreement. In professional partnerships, the main question that needs to be treated is how to value the interest of the deceased, and how to pay out his estate or his heirs. In many cases, this buy out is funded in whole or in part with life insurance that the partners carry on the lives of each other, or that the partnership carries on all its members. In others, there are complex buy-out patterns that are, in essence, the main reason for setting up the partnership in the first place. Even when the buy-out price is already known, or easy to establish, the manner of pay-out can have substantial significance. For example, if a portion of the price is a purchase of the deceased partner's ownership share, and a portion is his interest in partnership earnings, the distinction between these two segments can be quite meaningful.

It is in the area of the death buy-out formula, and the manner of establishing the price for the buy out that some of the most creative work has been done in recent years. Suppose, for example, that my only partner is my child, to whom I would be passing the largest part of my estate upon my death anyway. So I make him my partner, and establish a formula under which, in the event of the death of a partner, his estate is automatically bought out of the firm, leaving the surviving partner, my son, as the sole owner of the business. It is very important to me to have my estate valued as low as possible, in order to save on estate taxes, so I provide in the partnership agreement that my estate must sell my interest in the partnership for fifty cents, whether it's worth a million dollars or whatever. Then, my estate tax return shows that my partnership interest has a value of fifty cents, because that's the price at which it must be sold. Since my estate is in the 36% tax bracket, therefore, the tax owing is eighteen cents, instead of three hundred sixty thousand dollars, which would be the tax based on its real value of a million dollars.

Cute, huh? Yep. Too cute. It won't work. The same concept, however, shielded and fancied and complicated and enlarged upon, still provides some fertile fields for the estate planners to plow.

Setting a buy-out price, or, better, setting a buy-out formula way to establish a price, has many additional advantages, in addition to, or instead of, diddling the IRS out of a larger piece of the pie. For example, after Manny, Moe, and Jack have worked together for forty years, there is a basic trust and a sense of family that has developed among them. So, when Moe dies, Manny and Jack have a genuine concern. They also know that they are in top income tax brackets, and Moe's widow has no income at all. So, the way that they buy out Moe's estate can take advantage of this disparity. If they pay Moe's estate $100,000 for his interest in the company, they are paying it with after-tax dollars, and $100,000 is what Mrs. Moe gets. On the other hand, suppose that they buy his share for $20,000, but they also pay to her $30,000 a year for four years as an income continuation plan for the work Moe did before he died. Granted, Mrs. Moe will pay perhaps $2,500 a year in income taxes on the $30,000, leaving her a net of $27,500 times four, plus the original $20,000, or $130,000 instead of $100,000. Manny and Jack, who are in the 40% bracket, deduct the income continuation payments, saving $12,000 a year, so their total outlay is the original $20,000, plus four times $18,000, or $92,000 instead of $100,000. So, Manny and Jack have saved $8,000, and Mrs. Moe has received an extra $30,000, which she can really use, what with the kids in college and all.

Then too, there are partnerships where the firm itself is not tied to individual effort to the same extent as is the professional partnership. And that kind of partnership may be one where a partner would like to be able to transfer all or some of his interest to his family. So maybe the agreement should allow a partner to pass his interest to his immediate family. While there is a positive value to such a program in some cases, it's still true that a partner should be able to protect himself from waking up one morning and finding that his partner is no longer good old Mike, but now it's Mike's four kids, including the drunk, Mike's second wife who hasn't a brain in the world, and, worst of all, Mike's no good brother Charlie who can't keep his mouth shut about anything. Still, in some cases, there is a reason for a provision allowing some limited forms of transfer.

For example, let's imagine a partnership where the primary reason for existence is the ownership of income producing property, rather than providing a work environment for the partners. Let's suppose that we have a partnership which owns a tract of real estate and rents it out to others. There, the purpose of the partnership is a savings-building-unit, an estate planning device. One could well prefer, in a case of that nature, to provide in the partnership agreement that a partner may give or sell parts of his partnership interest to members of his family, or to trusts that he has created for the benefit of his family.

An example may help point out the value of this type of structure. Assume with me that I am a young physician, with a growing practice. I'd like to be able to pass along to my children some of the excess earnings that I am enjoying, but they, of course, are not licensed to practice medicine. So I buy a little office building for a price of $100,000, and I borrow $90,000 from the bank to buy it with. The bank takes a mortgage on the building to secure its $90,000 loan, so my equity in the building is $10,000. I give this equity to a partnership composed of my three children and my wife, so that each of them owns one-fourth of the building, and I have presented each of them with a gift, valued at $2,500, so there is no gift tax question raised. My medical practice pays rent to the partnership, and the partnership uses the rent to pay off the mortgage. The mortgage is designed to be paid out when my children go to college, and so the rent is then available for the kids to use at a time when they need everything they can get their hands on.

Partnerships of the investment ownership type may be just the thing for passing property rights from generation to generation, or for otherwise distributing family wealth, so it would be a bit undesirable to have such a structure terminate on the death of partner. Still, I don't want to end up in business with my partners' family, so I want to take advantage of some of those other devices we talked about earlier. Neither space, time, nor attention span permits an exhaustive list, but for starters, we could:

1. provide that on the death of a partner, his estate can accede to ownership, but not to decision-making power; or

2. provide that the heirs of a deceased partner can inherit his share, but they must limit active and personal participation to one person, who must be approved by the surviving partner; or

3. provide that if the heirs of the deceased partner want to stay involved in the property, they must offer to buy out the interest of the surviving partner if he wishes; or

4. provide for a system of evaluation of interests that will serve as an economic inducement to force the parties into a workable buy out in one direction or another.

A basic understanding of one simple rule of tax law is essential to decision making as it relates to partnerships. And that is this: as far as the folks at Internal Revenue are concerned, a partnership is nobody. That is: the partnership files an income tax return each year showing how much money it made, but it pays no tax. If A and B are equal partners, and the partnership earned $100,000, it is as though A earned $50,000 personally from his own business and B did the same. As noted above, however, A and B can have all sorts of strange formulas for splitting up the take between them. Essentially, any cockamamie scheme A and B can put together is OK with the Revenooers, so long as it has some connection with reality, so long as their total incomes equal the firm's total income, and so long as the firm follows through with what it claims that it is doing. A and B can have percentage ratios, or receive income shares based on initial investment, or divide it up according to ratios computed according to age, sex, hair color, waist measurement, or the square root of their social security numbers, but if that is what the partnership agreement actually provides, and if the partnership actually distributes its income in accordance with that formula, that's what each partner pays his income tax on, and that's the way the firm works.

This rule, as you can readily imagine, provides all sorts of openings for planning within a family. I can buy an apartment house and make my six-month-old daughter my partner. I do all the work, find the tenants, paint the apartments, fix the toilets, and cut the grass. But my teeny partner who isn't old enough to walk splits the take with me 50-50. Some folks are just born lucky.

THE LIMITED PARTNERSHIP

Of all the possible special arrangements, one is the subject of special statutory enactments, and deserves some special attention here. That is the limited partnership, which is a totally different animal from what we have been discussing so far.

You will remember that one of the shortcomings of the partnership was (and is) that every partner is personally liable for all the debts of the partnership. This means even the six-month-old daughter I told you about. All partners, whether in for 90% or one-tenth of 1%, are 100% responsible. That can get limiting, and even scary.

So a group of wise souls came up with the idea of the limited partnership, in which there are at least two classes of partners, general and limited. The general partner or partners have the same exposure as those in the normal, or general partnership. There are also, however, limited partners. These are persons who invest in the partnership in the same way persons buy stock in a corporation. Their entire investment is at risk (as in the case of a stockholder), but they have no responsibility beyond that point. They cannot be sued for the debts of the partnership. They cannot participate in running the business of the partnership, and they cannot play an active role in the firm. They are "limited" in all respects. But they can purchase their investment and sleep through the night without worry or concern about the Company. They are passive investors to an even greater extent than the small shareholder in a public corporation.

Many limited partnerships are rather large in scope and are run as investment vehicles—often public investment vehicles. But all the partners, general ones and limited ones, share in the income and loss according to the partnership agreement, and share in the proceeds when the partnership is dissolved.

A growing field in the area of complex estate planning is the family limited partnership, in which the general partner is daddy or a corporation controlled by daddy, and mom and the kids are limited partners. The agreement provides a system in which there is a gradual shifting of wealth to the kids and grandkids. Suffice it to say for these purposes that these are complicated devices which are in most cases to be used as a part of an all-inclusive sophisticated family structure designed by the family's attorney and accountant working in close concert.

Like the corporation, the limited partnership is formed by preparing an agreement among the partners and a certificate of limited partnership. It's possible, of course, that at the time of formation, one doesn't know who all the partners will be. These papers are signed, however, by at least one general partner and one limited partner. The agreement itself will provide for the addition of more partners, and will specify how others go about joining. Copies of a sample certificate and a sample agreement are attached as Appendixes D and E.

These documents are filed at the state capitol and in the county courthouse, similarly to the way one files documents that commence the life of a corporation. After they are filed, the entity is identified as a limited partnership, and has life. The documents are of public record, so that anyone can go to the courthouse, look them up, and learn the identity of at least some of the persons involved. The general partners have to be publicly known, of course, since those are the persons who are liable for all of the acts and omissions of the partnership. General partners in a limited partnership have the same exposure as partners in a general partnership; i.e., any one or all of the general partners can be stuck for any of the debts of the limited partnership.

Whenever a claim is asserted against the limited partnership, whether it be a claim for damages arising out of an automobile accident or a claim for last month's rent under a lease, the claimant can look to the partnership assets themselves, and then to the general partners and their assets. Where a limited partnership differs is that the limited partners have no personal liability for the partnership's obligations. Their personal assets are free from attack. The limited partner risks only what he has invested in the partnership, unless, of course, the limited partner signs personal guaranties or otherwise voluntarily makes further commitments for the benefit of the partnership.

It is this modest distinction, the addition of the element of partners who have no personal liability and no personal management right or responsibility which has permitted a limited partnership to grow to be a huge entity, with thousands upon thousands of limited partners and, on occasion, with millions upon millions of dollars of invested capital. Limited partnerships, like general partnerships, don't pay federal or state income taxes. The partnership agreement, in each case, specifies how the profits are distributed among the various partners, and each partner is taxed upon his share of the earnings. If the partnership has a loss, of course, each partner bears the specified portion of the loss and enjoys the income tax deductions that arise from it. It's necessary to emphasize, and perhaps to state it several times, that there is no necessary relationship between the number of dollars that a partner receives as spendable cash, from a partnership, on the one hand, and the number of dollars that he pays income taxes on for any given year. It is quite possible that, as a partner, I could be charged with thousands of dollars of income, as my share of the partnership earnings, and have not a penny to show for it. Nonetheless, I pay my taxes on those earnings, just as though they represented cash in my pocket. Similarly, it is very possible that I might have received thousands upon thousands of dollars in drawings and distributions from the partnership, and the partnership itself had a loss, so that not only do I have no taxes to pay, I have a deduction from my other income resulting from my share of the loss. In theory, eventually, of course, it all averages out, and paper losses get papered over with paper profits. The distinction, however, remains very viable, and forms a basis for some shrewd tax planning. It also provides another cause of April ulcers for the unwary.

One restriction on the ability of the limited partner to deduct losses needs to be mentioned. Even if the partnership has huge losses, a limited partner cannot deduct from his income an amount which exceeds the amount he has "at risk." What he has at risk is the sum total of what he has invested plus what his share of earnings have been plus whatever he is exposed to additionally upon the firm's debts. This amount is cumulative. So, if I invested $25,000 in the limited partnership, and I guaranteed $25,000 in debts of the Company, the most I can deduct in losses is $50,000. If I deduct $40,000 as my share of the partnership's losses in the first year, the most I can deduct thereafter (until the Company makes some money and adds it back to my capital account) is another $10,000. The balance just sits there, to be offset by future profits.

In summary, with partnerships generally, their greatest advantage is the ability to share the risk, the work, the responsibility, and the benefits with another. Similarly, their greatest disadvantage is a partner's obligation to be financially responsible for the debts and obligations and mistake of another.

The Inc. on the Bottom Line

A GENERAL DESCRIPTION

In our time, the quintessential form of business structure is the corporation. It deserves, therefore, a reasonably detailed description in these pages. In the days of good old Queen Elizabeth, a corporation was a creation of the crown. "Sir Walter Raleigh," quoth her majesty, "in return for introducing to the realm the quaint colonial custom of rolling up dried leaves, stuffing them into a pipe which you then set on fire and suck on, and thus cause lung cancer and all kinds of other snazzy stuff, we are granting to you a corporate charter. This document creates a new and different legal person, which you own, which can enter into all kinds of business (so long as it's within the scope of the charter), run up debts, buy and sell things, lease property, hire employees, and do almost anything that a living breathing human can do. And the neatest thing of all is that if the corporation fails to pay its debts, why the folks can sue the corporation, but they can't sue the shareholders. Isn't that neat?"

Well, that's not exactly the way it happened, but almost. A corporation, at first, existed only as the result of a specific enactment of the sovereign. In this country, that meant, generally, the State.

As the United States grew up, each state enacted its own corporation laws, because at common law (that is, under the system of court decisions, and precedents and the like) there can be no corporations except as specifically authorized by the statutes which the legislature enacted, and which, of course, the courts then interpreted. So, each state started out with the basic pattern that grew up under English law, and built its own system, as the devious legal minds of that state, and its basic political structure dictated. It provided general frameworks for the creation of corporations, rather than having each corporation especially and uniquely established by an action of the legislature. It assigned to a state official, usually the Secretary of State, the job of deciding whether an applicant had jumped through all the proper hoops. If so, the new corporation received a "charter," i.e., was born. It stands to reason that in states whose government was more beholden to (if not dominated by) large and strong and wealthy business corporations, the legislature found it to be a comforting way to behave to grant greater power to the corporation and, more important, to allow the corporation to do things which caused its controlling persons, its major shareholders and its directors, to hold and maintain concentrations of power. It is not surprising that the classic example of this approach was Delaware, which, at the time, was virtually the private preserve of the duPont family. Other states, more imbued with the opposite philosophy, such as Wisconsin, went in quite the opposite direction. This was why, for many years, the watchword for the incorporator who wanted to protect his hegemony over whatever came to pass was to incorporate in Delaware.

Today, and this by now comes as no surprise to you, the potbellied posse with the white hats, the guys who write the uniform statutes, have presented us with the Uniform Business Corporation Act, and most of the state legislatures have gone along with the idea. There are still notable state-to-state differences, but where we're discussing generally pervasive rules and ideas, so long as we pepper our conversation with "usually" and "in most cases" and "as a general rule," we can be reasonably universal in stating what the controlling law is.

So let's look at three things: (a) as structured today, what is the anatomy of a corporation; (b) how do you "do a corporation"; and (c) what can a corporation do? Our discussion relates primarily to the rules under the Uniform Business Corporation Act, or in the secret lingo of the initiated, the "BCA."

A corporation, once created under the laws of its home state, is a person. It can't breathe, and it has little need for a bathroom, but it can enter into contracts, pay taxes, buy and sell things, commit crimes and be punished, have children (called subsidiaries), grow wealthy, go broke, go bankrupt, move its residence, and cause fights in the family.

The basic instrument which gives the corporation birth is called the Articles of Incorporation. These Articles are contained in a document which provides for the name of the corporation, its home address, the types and amounts of stock which it can issue (more about that later), the persons who are its initial board of directors, and the name of the person in whose hands the sheriff slaps a summons on behalf of anyone who wants to sue the corporation. There are a number of other matters that go into the Articles as well, but they don't particularly concern us here and now.

For now, let's recognize that the Articles of Incorporation are a corporation's constitution and its birth certificate. While one could include in the Articles all kinds of limitations and restrictions, the better practice is usually to limit the Articles to providing what is required by statutes, and nothing more.

There are two reasons for the Articles being a "bare bones" document. First, the Articles are filed on record in the office of the Secretary of State, and in the courthouse of the county where the corporation makes its home. The Articles are public record, and anyone can go to the court house, read the articles, and get a copy. It's not hard to understand why it's more than just tacky to put into the articles that "Notwithstanding the fact that the only names in the articles are the lawyers who formed the corporation, the real guy behind the Company is old Joe Gotrocks who put two hundred thousand dollars of cash and that old warehouse down on Franklin Street into the company and he gave a fourth of the stock to his son-in-law."

Second, and just as important, once you have put rules into the Articles, the only way you can change them is to follow the procedure for amending set out in the statutes and in the Articles themselves, adopt amendments, and file them at the State Capitol and the County Courthouse with all the formalities that surrounded the original filing of the Articles themselves.

Years ago, there were requirements that a corporation have a measured finite life span ("Unless sooner dissolved, this corporation shall expire on the fiftieth anniversary of its formation, unless its life is then extended by an amendment to these articles."); that a corporation have at least three directors; and that at least one thousand dollars be paid in to the capital of the corporation before it was authorized to do business. These requirements each became more and more meaningless as time went by, and so they have now been omitted from statutory requirements in most states. For example, where the law required three directors, but only one person put up all the money, he named himself and two lackeys as directors. If either of the two directors was ever so thoughtless as to disagree with the boss, he was removed by a vote of the shareholders (all one of them, acting unanimously) and replaced with a new director who would have the common sense and good judgment always to vote with the boss. The extent of open discussion, unfettered debate and democratic rule was hardly sufficient to justify the retention of the three-director anachronism.

The other major document that spells out the life style of your corporation is the set of corporate bylaws that you adopt. Unlike the Articles of Incorporation, however, this time you can set your own ground rules. You may provide in the articles that the bylaws are to be promulgated only by the shareholders, or that they are to be written and adopted by the directors; you may or may not authorize directors to amend them. The one thing that you need to remember about all this is that the shareholders always have the right to amend the Articles of Incorporation, so the shareholders can change the ground rules about bylaws, just as they can change the ground rules about everything else, unless they have entered into a contractual relationship with each other renouncing this right.

Bylaws can govern activities of the corporation, down to some pretty minute details, or they can be broad stroke only. It's a matter of choice. At a minimum, however, bylaws should treat those questions. They should spell out the rights of shareholders and the procedures for shareholder meetings (when and where are the meetings held, who sends out the notices, how much notice is given, and so on). Bylaws prescribe the list of officers, how they are elected, what authority each one has, and who reports to whom. They can (but do not need to) provide who can sign checks, and how many signatures are needed. They provide when the fiscal year of the corporation begins and ends. Most important, they also provide how the bylaws are amended.

A corporation can also adopt other protocols of all sorts, if it wishes. Like other structures, it makes its own rules and, in many cases, it simply makes up the rules as it goes along. And, like other persons, sometimes it follows the rules it has set for itself, and sometimes it doesn't.

THE PRINCIPAL PLAYERS

There are four classes of persons who play roles in the life of a corporation, and an understanding of the process requires that one keep these classes separate, even though they are frequently composed of the same persons.

First, there are the shareholders. They are the ultimate owners of the corporation and the ultimate decision makers. There can be a number of classes of shareholders, with all different types of rights, but there must always be the very basic and ultimate class, the common shareholder, i.e., the owner of one or more shares of common stock. He has the right to vote (usually, one vote per share) and he has the final and terminal right to share in the assets on dissolution of the corporation. In other words, when the corporation is finally split up, if there are one hundred shares of common stock, the owner of each one gets one-one-hundredth of what's left after everybody else is paid off.

During the life of the corporation, if there is only the one class of common shares, each share has one vote in the election of directors, and one vote on each other matter presented for vote, and one vote on the question of whether the corporation should be dissolved. In addition, the shareholder has the right to one equal share of whatever dividends are declared by the board of directors. But, and this is an important "but," that's where a shareholder's rights as a shareholder end. As a shareholder, one isn't entitled to a job or a salary or a share of the profits or free insurance or anything else, just by reason of the fact that he is a shareholder. The one ongoing role that a shareholder, *as a shareholder,* has to play is the election of directors.

One of the more interesting aspects of corporate structure is the rule of cumulative voting, which in many states is mandated by statute and the articles may not provide otherwise. Simply stated, the rule is that whenever directors are being elected, each holder of voting stock receives a number of votes equal to the number of voting shares he holds, multiplied by the number of directors being elected. He has the right to "cumulate," i.e., to add together all those shares and vote them as a block for one candidate.

Here's why. If it were not for that rule, this is what could happen: The corporation, Big & Little, Inc., is having its annual meeting and electing a board of five directors. Of the 1,000 shares of Big & Little outstanding, John Big owns 600 shares and Mike Little owns 400 shares.

John announces the election of five directors. For the first director, John nominates himself and Mike nominates himself. They vote, and by a margin of 600 to 400 John is elected. Nominations for director #2 are opened. John nominates his wife, Marcie Big. Mike Little nominates himself. By vote of 600–400, Marcie Big is elected.

Nominations are opened for the third director. John Big nominates his son, John Big, Jr. Mike Little nominates himself. Guess what happens. And so it goes for all five directors.

Now, with cumulative voting, if there are five directors to be elected, John has 3,000 votes (i.e., 600 × 5) and Mike has 2,000 votes (i.e., 400 × 5). John nominates five members of the Big family, Mike nominates himself and his wife, and allocates 1,000 of his 2,000 votes to each. There is no way, arithmetically, that John can allocate votes among the five nominees from his family, or, indeed among any number of nominees to prevent a result in which Mike Little and his wife will be among the five candidates getting the largest number of votes. Therefore, the minority shareholder is guaranteed representation on the board of directors roughly commensurate with his proportionate holdings. As to what good it does one to get this minority representation on the board, that's another very interesting question.

I recall with some degree of amusement a shareholders' meeting of a corporation which I was serving as general counsel. There were some thirty or forty shareholders who attended the annual meeting. As counsel, I was seated at the head table, next to the President, so as to afford some guidance as to his permitted scope of authority if things got sticky.

The President of the Corporation introduced me and asked me to explain to the meeting the manner in which corporate shares are voted. I described the procedure in what seemed to me to be simple, clear, and persuasive terms, and sat down well pleased with myself.

The President asked if any of the shareholders present had any questions. There arose a somewhat wizened lady with close cropped gray hair, wire-rimmed glasses, a flower-print dress, and a black cane which she brandished as she spoke, like Stonewall Jackson wielding his sword as he urged and emboldened his troops.

"I got something to ax to him," she shouted, pointing her cane at me. Fortunately, I could see that the end of the cane was plugged and solid, so I felt no need to duck or take evasive action.

I stood up. "Yes, ma'am. I'll be happy to answer, if I can." My smile could have melted absolutely nothing.

"Young man," she said. (That demonstrates clearly that this incident took place many years ago, in the early-to-mid 1960's). "Are you telling me that if I have one hundred shares and that man over there "(again, pointing with the non-lethal but very demonstrative cane) "had two thousand shares, he gets twenty times as many votes as I have?"

"Yes, ma'am."

"On everything?"

"Yes, ma'am."

"No matter what?"

"Yes, ma'am."

"Young man, don't you have any idea at all what democracy is, what our boys in Khaki fought and died for, all men are created equal, one nation indivisible with liberty and justice for all?"

"Yes, ma'am."

She swung her cane around a bit and glared right through me and out the back of my head. "Well I never," she said as she sat down. And then, in a comment to her neighbor loud enough to be heard several blocks away, "That black-headed one there at the table, he's a comm-a-nist or something, you mark my words."

Years later, and notwithstanding the unquestionable patriotism of that lady, I feel obligated to continue to advise that you get one vote for every voting share you own—no more and no less.

The Articles will generally provide either that the shareholders write the bylaws, or that the directors write the bylaws. The bylaws spell out the procedures by which the directors are elected. Frequently in the small or "closely held" corporation, either the Articles or the bylaws provide that each year the shareholders will decide how many directors will compose the board for the coming year, and that an entire new board will be elected each year. Remember, of course, that there is small reason indeed to mourn for the limited power of the shareholder, for several reasons: first, a shareholder who has enough shares to do so will normally elect himself a director; second, a shareholder who isn't totally satisfied with what the director does elects a new and more amenable director; and, third, of course, the shareholder is the one who gave the corporation life, and who can end that life as well.

A huge number of variations has come to exist on the types of shares, and the rights inherent in shares. The simplest and the earliest is the distribution between common stock and preferred stock. Classically, preferred stock (1) had no right to vote, (2) was entitled to a specified dividend, and (3) received a specific preference on dissolution of the corporation. For example, a share of preferred stock might be "$100.00 par, 6% cumulative dividend stock." This meant that the initial investment at the time of purchase of the share of stock was $100.00, and in return for that, the stockholder was entitled to receive $6.00 per share dividend each year. This dividend would be payable out of the profits of the corporation before any dividends were paid to common shareholders. Since dividends are payable only out of profits or retained earnings, and only if the directors declare them, there would be a possibility that the dividend would not be paid, but if it should be skipped one year, the stock was "cumulative" so the shareholder would be entitled next year to receive $12.00 before any moneys went to the common shareholders. And so on. The "$100.00 par value" meant that when the corporation was dissolved, the holder of the preferred shares would get $100.00 for each share before the common shareholder got anything. But, on the other hand, that's all he would get, no matter how big and successful the company became. The common shareholder had all the leverage and took all the risk.

The common shareholder, in earlier days, often had a "par value" tag on his shares too, usually indicative of the amount the share sold for when first issued. In his case, however, the "par" didn't mean much; his ownership was one fractional share of the residual worth of the corporation, whatever it happened to be.

Then along came the bells and whistles, infinite in number. One example was "participating preferred" where the holder received his six-dollar dividend plus an additional amount equal to whatever the holder of the common shares received—or equal to a stated portion of what the common shareholder received, or whatever.

There were issues of preferred stock which carried the right to vote—or which carried the right to vote on certain very important issues only—or which carried the right to vote only when the dividends were in arrears, or the like.

Then came the corporation with various classes of stock—Class A and Class B and Class XYZ. Each class would have a specific list of rights, differing from each other class.

In some cases, Class A stock and Class B stock would each have the right to vote on all matters, but Class A stock would have the right to elect eight of the twelve directors and Class B stock would have the right to elect the other four directors. This could be done even if there were only one thousand Class A shares and one hundred thousand Class B shares. In other words, it was primarily the Class A shareholders who had essential control of the Company and they intended to keep it that way.

An additional characteristic sometimes accorded to preferred stock is to make it "convertible." That is, we allow the holder of a preferred share to trade it in for a common share whenever he wishes. When the business of the corporation appears sufficiently successful to the preferred shareholder, he gives up his preferred right to $6.00 in dividends each year and his preferred right to the first $100.00 on liquidation in return for the uncertain but (he decides) more valuable right to share in the open-ended dividend right of the common shareholder, and the open-ended right for one fractional share of whatever the corporation is sold for, together with the right to vote.

Of the "tacked-on" perks that shares sometimes carry with them, one of the most popular is the warrant. Here's how it works: the corporation gives each shareholder (for example) the right to buy additional new shares from the corporation for $10.00 each at the rate of one new share for each two shares that he owns. Thus, if you have one hundred shares, you have the right to buy up to fifty more shares for a total of $500.00. Usually, you also have the right to sell the warrants and transfer them while keeping the stock.

With smaller corporations today, the trend (and in some states, the rule, under current versions of the BCA) is for there no longer to be "common" stock and "preferred" stock—there's just "stock." Some shares may have one group of characteristics (i.e., package of rights to vote, to receive dividends, etc.) and other shares have quite a different group, but they're all just "stock." The groups of shares may or may not be classified as "Class A" and "Class B."

To get back to our story and our cast of characters, however, let's remember that it's the voting shareholders who elect the directors.

And, please, let's dispel one more rather painful misnomer. Each person elected is a "Director." The group of them, together, constitute the "Board of Directors." One person in that group is not a "Board of Director." He is a Director.

It is the board of directors of the corporation who make the basic decisions of how a corporation will act, what it will do, what officers it will have and who they will be, and so forth and so on. The board elects corporate officers to carry out the policies and instructions given by the board, but these officers have only the authority to do what the board tells them to do. The officers are the implementers; the directors are the deciders. It is the directors, for example, who decide (in theory) how many persons are to be employed, how they are to be compensated, and what they are to do. The officers find the employees and hire them.

Every corporation has at least two officers, a President and a Secretary, although sometimes they can be the same person. The corporation can have as many additional officers as the bylaws suggest. There can be Vice Presidents, and Treasurers, and Managers, and Assistants, and a Chairman of the Board. There are corporations with Chaplains and Coaches and Chairmen and Chairwomen and just plain Chairs. One of the more fraudulently maintained corporations in Kentucky's history had a Chief Chaplain and Two Assistant Chaplains. Generally, the role of an officer is whatever the bylaws specify the role is, and the duties are whatever the bylaws say they are.

The Employees constitute the fourth class of persons associated with the corporation. Each employee has a contractual relationship with the corporation, and the terms of that contract, written or spoken or understood and tacit, determine the whole relationship.

One distinction needs to be pointed out in the composition of these groups, the shareholders, the directors, the officers, and the employees. The latter three, directors, officers, and employees, are always composed of living breathing humans. Shareholders, on the other hand, can be humans, or partnerships, or trusts, or other corporations. Together, the group make up the anatomy of a corporation.

CREATING THE CORPORATION

How do we give birth to one of these persons? The birthing process is sanitary, immediate, nonthreatening, and without suspense. The parents have total control over the baby's sex, size, abilities, and lifestyle. And they can maintain the same degree of control as their baby grows up. A virtual parent's dream, what?

Articles of Incorporation, which we have already described, are signed and notarized and sent to the office of the Secretary of State. A corporation clerk in that office determines whether the selected name is or is not available, i.e., whether it is or is not deceptively similar to an existing name. Once that hurdle is surmounted, there are only two questions to be checked: Do the Articles contain the essential provisions spelled out in the statute, and is there a check attached for the filing fees? If those two rather simple tests are met, the Articles are filed, stamped, and returned to the Incorporator.

A sample set of Articles of Incorporation is attached as Appendix A at page 131.

The Incorporator, by the way, is simply the person or persons who signed the Articles. He may be the persons who are the moving parties, the "parents" of the new baby, or he may be the attorney who wrote the Articles. It really doesn't matter, because his role is a very limited one. As soon as the first meeting takes place, the Incorporator turns control over to the shareholders, who elect the directors, and so on.

At any rate, when the Incorporator receives the Articles back from the Secretary of State, he records them in the courthouse of the county where the corporation resides, and the formation is complete.

The next step is the opening meeting. In theory, it takes place in stages, although in practice what we have is a simultaneous signing of several pieces of paper.

The Articles have appointed an initial Board of Directors, who have their opening meeting. They determine the characteristics of the stock, and they sell the opening issue of shares, for the prices and on the terms that they specify. The opening board of directors adopt bylaws (or, in some cases, they pass the buck to the shareholders), and they throw the control of the entity to the shareholders who just bought the stock.

The newly constituted group of shareholders, voting within the scope of the bylaws, elect a board of directors. Wonder of wonders, it's usually precisely the board named in the articles. This board meets, elects officers, sets up some ground rules like who can sign checks and the like, and gets the business started.

At this point, let's draw a comparison or two. In a sole proprietorship, the capital, the basic wealth, the wherewithal that the proprietor has to draw upon as a source of credit or purchasing strength, consists of everything that that proprietor owns. That is the capital of his business and, undifferentiated, it is the capital of his person.

The partnership has as its capital whatever the partners have contributed as capital to the partnership. Once

Partner A puts in his cash, and Partner B puts in his credit, and Partner C puts in her property, and Partner D puts in her designs, these are all, collectively, the undifferentiated properties of the partnership. But, because the partnership doesn't have that special "person-ness" under the law, a claim made against the partnership is also made against all of the partners as individuals, and their individual separate properties which they never contributed to the partnership are also available for response to the claims of outsiders. This uncontributed property (my house, my car, any life insurance, my piano, etc.), however, does not become part of the partnership's "capital," even though it is at risk.

It is by comparison to these two described situations that the uniqueness of the corporation stands out. The corporation's capital consists of what the stockholders have paid to the corporation for their stock, and of whatever else the corporation earns or, in some manner, acquires. And that's the sum total of what's available for the grab of creditors or claimants. The stockholders have subjected to risk what they chose to subject, and nothing more. If the corporation fails, the stockholder has lost his investment in the stock of the corporation and whatever else he chose to put at risk; nothing more.

Of course, like everything else, there's a lot more to the story. First, as a general rule, when you and I put in a hundred bucks each and form our corporation, we're going to find it a little short on credit. After all, how much credit would you extend to a one-week-old baby with two hundred dollars? So, what happens is the demand for personal guarantee. The landlord says, "I'll rent the store to the corporation, but, Lady, you gotta guarantee the lease personally." The banker says, "Sure I'll give you a five thousand dollar line of credit, but you'll have to either put up some collateral or guarantee it yourself." So it happens that some personal exposure comes into play. But the basic rule still obtains, and there is no personal liability, except where one has intentionally and knowingly signed a piece of paper expressing the guarantee. And guarantees can be limited as to time and as to amount, and, after some time goes by, and the corporation lives and grows, it needs less and less to have guarantees to back it.

So now we have the corporation established, and it has one shareholder (that's you), and a board of directors consisting of one person (that's you), and a President and Secretary, both of whom are you. The corporation has entered into one employment contract, and that is also with you. Dissent among the shareholders, directors, officers, and employees is virtually nonexistent. Thus constituted, how does it operate? Well, other than the fact that most corporate meetings take place in the bathroom in front of the mirror, it operates in the same basic and essential way as General Motors.

The shareholders prescribe the ground rules and, to whatever extent they choose to do so, they spell out in bylaws or protocols the scope of activity permitted to the directors and officers. The shareholders elect the directors, and the directors run the Company.

A sample set of bylaws is at Appendix B, page 135.

The directors, operating on a one director-one vote basis, set policy, elect the officers, and specify policy and plans, within the scope of the framework the shareholders spelled out.

The officers, whose job descriptions are outlined in the bylaws, and the one or a thousand or a million other employees who fill out the table of organization do the work of the company.

There's another whole set of rules that come into play when we look into your bringing others in as shareholders in your corporation.

As we've already noted in other context, the law frequently works on the principle of static inertia. What I mean by that is this: In virtually every case, there is the general rule, and then there are all of the exceptions. Often, it is the exceptions which provide the prevalent situation, and it is easy to forget that, whether applying in the majority of cases or not, they are still the exceptions. The highways belong to the state, and absolutely nobody has the right to drive a car on them. Unless he has a license, granted to him under the rules prescribed by the state.

No one is guilty of having committed a crime. Unless and until a jury of his peers has marched back into the courtroom from the jury room and pronounced that they have found him guilty.

I own a beautiful flat half acre of land, right in the city, close to schools and close to shopping. I may not, however, under any circumstances build a house on it. Unless and until I get myself a building permit.

A similar type of static inertia applies to the general rules with respect to the sale of stock by corporations. The basic rule is that no corporation can issue stock at anytime to anybody without full registration of the offering with the securities department of every state in which the stock is being offered for sale, and with the Securities and Exchange Commission in Washington. Then come the exceptions. The exceptions are many, and are complex, and it is not the purpose of this discussion at this point to give you a full and reliable checklist of the exceptions. For our purposes, however, let's first note that until you are offering your stock in the millions of dollars in several states, to dozens of people, you are probably not a big enough fish for the Securities and Exchange Commission to be concerned with.

The threshold of concern with the State Department of Securities, however, is a much lower one. Like the Feds, the state grants all kinds of exemptions from the need for registration, but the state also provides, by statute, that even if your transaction or your security is the sort that is exempted, you don't have the exemption unless you have filed an application for it and have been granted it. Here, we are speaking of the exemptions that are available to the security offerings of less than $200,000, or security offerings made all in the same state to residents of the same state to no more than 25 persons, or security offerings made in connection with an agreement entered into by ten or fewer people, all of whom have gotten together for the purpose of forming the company, and the formation of the company is a mutual endeavor of the entire group. Certainly, the smallest of "offerings," that is, the capitalization of a corporation by one person who forms his own company and puts his money into it, is exempted under any of these tests.

The cautionary words to remember, from this discussion, are these: Where a business is being started or acquired by an individual or a very small group, and stock is to be offered to and sold to and issued to the members of that very small group, an exemption is available. In most instances, other than a one-man show, it is a good idea to apply for and receive a confirmation of the exemption, or at least to have some intelligent discussion and consideration of the question whether an application for the exemption is pertinent in the case.

What happens if you are entitled to an exemption, but do nothing to secure it? Probably nothing. Whether I have insurance or not, my house probably won't burn down this year. But I buy fire insurance anyway.

Having secured your exemption letter, and capitalized your corporation, and elected your directors and officers, your corporation is alive and well. On its behalf you apply for federal and state identification numbers, you open bank accounts, and you purchase what you need to start in business. You document your purchases, and your purchases are all discussed and considered and approved by the board of directors of your corporation, even if the board is only you. And if you have bought these assets from yourself, you are still certain to document the purchases, and to record them as transfers from the previous owners to the corporation.

THE JOY OF TAXATION

One of the first decisions that you have to make nowadays when you begin this operation is whether you are going to be a C corporation or an S corporation. This requires a little bit of conversation and little bit of explanation.

First, let's dispel the smoke screen. Essentially, there isn't any difference between a C corporation and an S corporation. Each of them is a corporation, and each one has the same characteristics, shareholders, directors, officers, records, minute books, problems, and the like. The only difference is that the S corporation has filed a specific form with the Internal Revenue Service stating that it wants to be an S corporation. Under the static inertia rule that we discussed above, every corporation starts off as a C corporation. Every corporation remains a C corporation until and unless it elects to be an S corporation. A corporation which has only one class of shares, which has 75 or fewer shareholders, none of which shareholders are other corporations or trusts (except for certain specific types of trusts), can elect to be an S corporation. (Like other discussions in this little book where tax considerations come into play, there are specific exceptions to virtually all of the rules mentioned. The S corporation rules are also that way, so assume, for the time being, that these are just general statements, not absolutes.) All of the shareholders sign a printed form declaring their decision, the form is filed with Internal Revenue Service during the first seventy-five days of a year, and we have an S corporation.

Once a corporation becomes an S corporation, it stays an S corporation until it disqualifies itself (such as by having 76 or more shareholders) or files a paper saying it has decided to revert to C corporation status. Once a corporation changes from S to C, voluntarily or involuntarily, it must remain a C corporation for at least five years before it can go back to being an S corporation.

The difference between the C corporation and the S corporation is that the S corporation pays no taxes. The shareholders, instead, pay the taxes on the S corporation's income. If you own 10% of the stock of the S corporation, and the corporation has earnings of $75,000, 10% of that sum, or $7,500, shows up on your income tax return. If somebody else owns 20% of that corporation, $15,000 shows up on his income tax return. And so all of the income is accounted for, it's just paid on the tax returns of the stockholders rather than the corporation. Similarly, if the S corporation has a loss instead of a profit, each of the shareholders has for a deduction on his income tax return his proportionate share of the loss. The shareholders of an S corporation are treated, for tax purposes, like partners in a partnership.

The basic advantages of the S corporation are these: Almost every business has a loss during its first year of operation. If the shareholders have to put up the money, they can derive some comfort from their investment by having the corporation's loss to deduct on their income tax returns. Later, when the corporation has been around long enough to earn a profit, the corporation can change from an S corporation to a C corporation, and the individuals no longer have to pay the taxes. Another advantage of the S corporation is this: When the taxes have been paid on the S corporation's income, that income can be distributed to the shareholders without any further tax. Compare this to the normal corporation which earns money, pays income tax on it, and then has accumulated profits. If the profits are distributed to the shareholders, that is a dividend, and the shareholders again pay tax on the money. So, for example, assume that the top $1,000 of corporate income of a C corporation is subjected to a 35% tax, and so after paying the tax, the corporation has $650 left. Assume that the corporation then decides to pay that $650 as a dividend to its shareholders, who have 40% income tax brackets of their own to concern themselves with, so when they receive the $650 dividend, they pay another $260 of it as income tax, and there is only $390 left. If, on the other hand, the corporation had been an S corporation, and had earned that top $1,000, the shareholder in the 40% bracket would have paid his $400 tax on the $1,000, and had $600 left to spend on his vacation.

Is it always that simple? Of course not. Like everything else, there are all sorts of complications that enter into the calculations. Otherwise, every corporation that could qualify as an S corporation would do so. And obviously they don't. Why don't they? For one thing, there are some corporations which may earn the profit, and have the taxable income, but don't have the cash to distribute to the shareholders by way of dividend or otherwise. Perhaps the corporation needs to keep the money on hand to pay for its equipment, or to expand. The shareholder reasons that if there is no way to distribute the money to him anyway, he would just as soon have the corporation keep the profit and be taxed at

35% as distribute the profit to him on the books only, and have him pay the 40%. Perhaps the corporation is operating in an area where it is essential to it to enhance its net worth by internal growth, so that it can qualify for credit or for bonding or whatever. The reasons for making one choice or another are many, and each situation stands on its own. The important thing here is only to be aware of the fact that there is a choice that can be made.

The C corporation, remember, is a taxable person in its own right. Annually it calculates its income, subtracts its deductions, and pays its own income taxes. It makes estimates for the current year, and pays quarterly installments, like humans do. Its tax brackets are slightly different from that of humans, ranging from 15% (on income below $25,000) to 35% (on income over $100,000).

From the shareholder's standpoint, the important fact to remember is that a C corporation's retained earnings—its income after taxes—stays in the corporation until it is paid out to shareholders as a dividend and, at that time, it's income to the shareholder, so he pays tax on it again. That's the reason that the S corporation was initiated in the first place.

This is a good time while talking income and taxes to lay before you another of those piercing glimpses into the obvious. That's this: Income is not a cigar box full of greenbacks waiting to be enjoyed. Income is a legal concept, a calculation, a number of dollars reached by computing revenues (which may or may not be represented by cash, and may just as easily be reflected in accounts receivable or notes or other things) reduced by expenses (which may or may not represent cash outlays, and can just as easily, and will in many cases be represented by computed depreciation, or booked accounts payable or other things). What's left is "income." Maybe it's something to spend and maybe not; all that is certain is that it is something used to measure income taxes, and those, invariably, are payable in cash whether the cash is there or not.

One further word about taxes before we leave the subject. Like all other employees, a corporation pays wages to its employees, and it deducts from those wages a contribution to social security, federal income taxes, state income taxes, and city occupation taxes. Those deductions should be (but sometimes are not) actually extracted whenever payroll is paid, and set aside for delivery to Federal, State, and local taxing authorities. The amounts withheld are referred to by the tax folks as "trust fund" taxes. In other words, when I pay an employee $500.00 in wages, but all he gets is $400.00 because I withhold the other $100.00, I am personally obligated to set that $100.00 aside and send it to my friendly tax collectors. The key word in the sentence you just finished reading is "personally."

This is the one exception to the general rule that I am not personally responsible for any of the debts of my corporation. Generally, as we have noted, the reason for having a corporation is to insulate the entrepreneur—the shareholder—from personal liability for any corporate debt. But here, well, you see, you hafta' see it this way: The same guys who own the Courthouse and pay the judge's salary are the guys who collect taxes. So there's a different rule. (It's like Internal Revenue sends you letters without buying stamps because those same guys also own the Post Office.)

In this limited area of operation, that of employment tax withholding, if the corporation fails to send in the money withheld from the employees, the fellow in charge of the corporation books and accounts and payroll gets stuck with a penalty for not honoring his trust fund obligations to hold that money out and send it to the government. And how much is that penalty? You guessed it. It's whatever amount you were supposed to withhold and send in. Exactly.

THE DEATH OF THE CORPORATION

Like all other living beings, a corporation can reach the end of its life span. Maybe there simply is no further market for monogrammed buggy whips. Maybe the three chums who started the business have simply decided to close it down and retire, and they want to cash in on the fruits of their efforts over these many years. Or maybe there simply isn't any demand anymore for a Chinese hand laundry. At any rate, the time comes for the termination of the corporation.

Some corporations, of course, slide down the slippery slope and end up bankrupt. That would be a tragic way to die, but it happens to corporations, as well as to others. When that takes place the entire process is conducted in the federal courts, and with procedures that aren't part of this discussion. In other cases, without bankruptcy, the corporation simply goes out of business, runs out of assets, and stops breathing. If no reports are filed for a couple of years, the Secretary of State, at the state capitol, allows the corporation to be "administratively dissolved" and like Puff, the Magic Dragon, it simply slides beneath the waves and is heard from no more.

When a corporation has built a store of assets, however, and the time comes for its dissolution, there are specific procedures to take. First, the directors make a decision to liquidate and dissolve the corporation and generally they make this recommendation to the shareholders. The shareholders meet, gravely consider the terminally ill body of the corporation, and decide to pull the plug. The shareholders vote to dissolve, and the death process sets in.

The persons in charge of liquidation "reduce" the assets to cash. That is to say, generally, they sell the inventory and the equipment and the machinery and whatever else the corporation owns. Next they pay all the debts of the corporation, and cancel all of its relationships and contracts. The amount of money left in the till, therefore, if there is any, belongs to the shareholders, and it is divided up among them as a liquidating dividend. Each shareholder receives his proportionate piece of the pie, and articles of dissolution are signed and filed in the state capitol. The life cycle has come to an end.

In some cases, of course, the corporation itself may cease to exist, but some aspect of its business continues. Sometimes, one or more aspects of the business may be sold to shareholders, or distributed to shareholders in lieu of cash. In other words, if A owns a third of the corporation, the corporation has $300,000 in assets, and $100,000 of these assets are delivery trucks which the corporation used in its business, Shareholder A, with the agreement of the corporation and the other shareholders, takes the delivery trucks, paints his own name on them, and receives them in return for his shares. The same thing could take place when a corporation has an ongoing business activity which is sold to one of the shareholders, for cash, or for shares, by agreement of all parties, as part of the liquidating process. In other words, when the assets are sold off, as the sun sets, it is not always essential that they be sold to strangers. Sometimes the members of the family itself can find the best use for, and therefore pay the best price for, some of these assets. At any rate, each shareholder has received the same dollar value for each share held by him. This revenue is treated in the same way as the proceeds from the sale of a listed stock. The shareholder has either a capital gain or a capital loss, which he reports to his accountant, who dutifully records it for the edification of our friends at Internal Revenue.

And you, the stockholder, take off to seek greener and newer fields in which to play.

5

LLC, The New Kid on the Block

In very recent years, a new form of business structure has emerged. Unlike the partnership and the corporation, this is an entirely new device, created to serve current needs, in a world where the functioning cause is the changing requirements of the Internal Revenue Code, rather than the historical evolution of the common law through case precedent. This spanking new device is the Limited Liability Company, or as the boys in the back room call it, the LLC. Originating in other countries, primarily Germany, where it is referred to as a "GmbH," it came to the United States originally in the 1970s. When the Internal Revenue Service confirmed in a 1988 ruling that it would recognize this new device, and accept it for taxation as a partnership (see discussion below), the states began, one by one, to adopt statutes permitting the structure to exist and operate. By early 1994, well over thirty states had fallen into line, and it followed as the night the day that the rest of the states have now adopted enabling legislation, Hawaii being the last, in early 1966.

The phenomenon of the growth of this new type of structure in a matter of months, while partnerships and corporations have each developed over a span of five hundred or more years, demonstrates several unrelated conditions of the business world as it exists at the end of the twentieth century. First, it serves as another indication of the facts that the United States is no longer a confederation of fifty neighboring but independent legal and economic structures, and that the world is no longer an assembly of a number of neighboring but independent sovereign legal and economic entities. Second, it is a remarkable case study of the speed with which fifty independent cantankerous state legislatures, each with carloads of political and financial baggage, can act to adopt similar, if not identical, new laws of extraordinarily far-reaching impact upon the business community, without extended years of committee evaluation, without reports from legislative research organizations, formal or informal, lobbyist-backed or governmental, and without a significant degree of understanding in the minds of many of the members of the legislature of exactly what it is that they are enacting. Golly, Mike, if the folks in Oregon and Florida and Vermont figured it was a good thing, I guess we oughta do it, too.

What is an LLC? Well, the easy description is to call it sort of a cross between a partnership and a corporation. It is that, but such a description does you no good at all. It's the kind of answer that reminds one of one of the better lawyer-bashing stories that have earned such popularity.

Two friends were out for a ride in a hot air balloon, when the prevailing air currents took them far off their expected course, and over a region that was totally unfamiliar to them. They were lost. They brought the balloon lower, to get within earshot of the ground, and they noticed a man standing in a field.

"Hey, there," shouted one of the balloonists to the man on the ground, "Can you help us?"

"Sure, I can," responded the man in the field.

"Can you tell us where we are?" shouted the balloonist.

"Sure," said the earthbound fellow again. "You're up there in a balloon."

One balloonist turned to the other and said, "That man down there is a lawyer."

"How can you tell that?" asked his colleague.

"Well," came the response, "you asked him a simple question. The answer you got was directly responsive and to the point, it was completely accurate, and it was totally worthless."

So maybe there is a definition of the LLC which is of a bit more value, or, at least, not totally worthless. An LLC is a legal person, an independent entity, created by persons who satisfy specific statutory requirements. It can sue and be sued; it can buy, sell, own and deal with property; it can enter into contracts and obligations of all kinds; and it can engage in business in the same manner as any other person. Anyone, a human, a corporation, a partnership, a trust, even another LLC, can be a member of the LLC if the controlling documents so provide.

The key word, the operative relationship in an LLC is the "member." Partnerships have partners; corporations have stockholders; LLC's have members. The members are the owners, the deciders, and usually the guys who run the show.

As with a corporation or a limited partnership, the formal act that creates an LLC is the filing of a document with the Secretary of State. Here, the document is called "Articles of Organization." These articles, which can later be amended, just as a corporation's articles of incorporation can be amended, specify the name of the LLC, its address, its registered agent (that's the person who is authorized to receive important documents, such as summonses and subpoenas, on behalf of the LLC), an affirmation (in most states) that the LLC has at least two members, and, most important, whether it is to be run by its members or by a manager. It does not need to tell who its members are, or who its manager is, or what business it expects to engage in, unless it is a professional LLC.

A brief aside: The professional LLC, or the PLLC, is a slightly different bird, in that it is created for the practice of a specific profession of a sort that can be practiced only by licensed practitioners, such as physicians, or lawyers, or accountants, or architects, or psychologists, or the like. Only persons who are licensed to practice the profession that the PLLC is established for may be members, and, presumably, the name of the PLLC and the Articles of Organization do disclose what type of business it is involved in.

As noted above, the Articles of Organization of an LLC are nothing more than a statement to the world at large that the LLC exists. The more critical instrument is the "Operating Agreement." This agreement is analogous to the partnership agreement in a partnership, and to the bylaws and minutes and agreements that form the backbone of a corporation.

The Operating Agreement defines who the members are, and what each has contributed to the company. If the LLC is one run by a manager, the Operating Agreement can identify the manager, spell out the authority which the manager has and provide what the manager gets for doing his managing. It also can provide how the manager is elected and how the manager is replaced. The manager, by the way, doesn't have to be a human being; a corporation, a partnership, a limited partnership, or even another LLC can be the manager.

Where the articles specify that the LLC has a manager, no member has the right, just by virtue of being a member, to bind the LLC on any contract. In that situation, being a member of an LLC is like being a shareholder in a corporation. Unless otherwise provided in either the articles or the Operating Agreement (and virtually anything can be provided there), the manager is elected by a majority vote of the members. Absent any provision to the contrary, a manager is liable to the LLC or to the members only for wanton or reckless misconduct, and conduct has to get pretty bad before it is classified as wanton or reckless. Mere negligence, no matter how blatant, doesn't do it.

Of course, where the manager is an outsider, a hired hand, either the articles, or the Operating Agreement, or the contract between the LLC and the manager can specify in detail what the manager's responsibilities are, and what the manager's liabilities are, what is expected of him, or her, or it, and what can happen if those expectations are not met. Remember our previous discussion of inertia in the law; it is the role of the general law here just to spell out what the rules are where the parties have not adopted their own rules. This not only removes the uncertainty; it also serves as a powerful stimulus to face issues, come up with your own answers, and codify them into an agreement.

On the other hand, in those cases where the Articles of Organization do not provide for a manager, but, rather, provide that the members themselves shall operate the LLC, then any member can bind the LLC in the same way that any partner can bind a partnership.

In that case, being a member is more like being a partner, except that the member has no personal liability for the acts and obligations of the LLC. Remember the partnership discussion in this context. A member of an LLC who acts to bind the LLC when the LLC itself hasn't given him the authority to do so can be required to respond very pragmatically to the other members of the LLC and to the LLC itself. It's only with respect to the outsider that his efforts to bind the LLC have been successful. That is, when the unauthorized member of a member-managed LLC has entered into an agreement for the LLC to buy ten green ones and ten blue ones, the seller of the blue ones and the green ones is entitled to be paid by the LLC. The unauthorized member is still stuck with the job of answering to the other members and of paying the LLC for his indiscretion.

Unless specific rules to the contrary have been entered into, a majority of the members of an LLC can cause the LLC to do virtually anything, except to amend the Articles of Organization or the Operating Agreement, or to authorize an act which is in violation of the Articles of Organization or the Operating Agreement. Those take unanimous action. Always, to change an LLC from one controlled by the members to one controlled by a manager, or vice versa, requires the unanimous consent of the members.

The Operating Agreement can contain any terms that the members agree upon for the proportions in which the profits of the operation are distributed to members, or in which the assets will be divided upon dissolution of the entity. If there are no provisions made, the division among members is equal.

There is a long list of events, any one of which will bring about the automatic dissolution of a LLC, although statutes generally provide that the automatic dissolution occurs upon the happening of the described event, unless otherwise provided in the written Operating Agreement, or unless continuity is authorized by a unanimous consent of all members. These terminating events include the death or incompetence or bankruptcy of any member, or the resignation and withdrawal of a member. Thus, in the absence of a written agreement to the contrary, one member's voluntary act of withdrawal can result in a very significant taxable event to all the other members. That, in itself, should provide a huge impetus to covering those matters in the Operating Agreement.

One of the major differences between the LLC and the corporation is in the transferability of interests. Generally unless the Operating Agreement provides for something else a member cannot sell or transfer his interest at any time to any person under any circumstances without the unanimous consent of all other members. In some circumstances, if a member attempts to sell or assign his interest, he can transfer good title, but this is a "disassociation" and unless every one of the other members has consented and accepted the transferee as a new replacement member within 90 days, the LLC automatically dissolves. Some of the states which have established the LLC recently (Nevada, for example) have provided that the attempted transfer can take place without dissolving the LLC, but the transferee, if he is not accepted by all the other members, gets only a monetary and profit interest, and gets no vote or voice in control of the organization. In years to come, there will undoubtedly be court interpretations of such a bizarre rule; for now, we can only wonder at it and ask hypothetical questions.

The main reason for the establishment of the LLC as a new vehicle was to fill a gap among the partnership, the C corporation, and the S corporation. Remember, there are only two operational taxing schemes for the business entity. The C corporation computes its own income, takes its own deductions, and pays taxes on its net. For the most part, if the humans who own the corporation want to get some of the profits into their own pockets, they have to cause the corporation to declare dividends and pay them. The dividends are not deductible to the corporation, but they are taxable to the recipients as their income.

Partnerships, on the other hand, don't pay income tax. They report their income to their partners (whether they distribute it to them or not) and the partners each pay tax on the portion of the income assigned to each. The S corporation bridged this gap to a substantial extent, by allowing certain corporations to elect to be taxed as though they were partnerships, but there are strict limits on S corporations. They can't have more than 75 shareholders, they can't have nonresident alien shareholders, they can't have corporations or trusts (except for a special type of qualified trust) as shareholders, and they can't be engaged in certain businesses.

Now, the state legislatures cannot tell the Internal Revenue Service how to treat a business entity for income tax purposes, but they can prescribe what kind of business entities can exist. They have, therefore, created a new animal to fit within these rules, and that's the LLC. As noted above, an entity can be treated in only one of two ways, as a corporation (pay its own taxes) or as a partnership (divide its income among the owners, and each of them pays tax on his share). It takes no great stretch of the imagination to realize that there needs to be some kind of test as to whether a given entity is to be put into one group or another, to be taxed as a corporation or as a partnership; otherwise, those running a particular business would provide whatever kinds of ground rules they choose, and then call it a partnership, or call it a corporation, and that's how it would be taxed.

There is no way that our Federal friends would leave an opening like that. If nature abhors a vacuum, Internal Revenue not only abhors it, it despises, condemns, hates, and is completely and pathologically obsessed at the idea of, a vacuum. IRS asks the courts to fill in all the holes with case law, and then issues regulations, rulings, procedures and the like to fill in the spaces. So here, on this matter, we have an explicit answer to the question of how do you decide whether a business is to be taxed as a corporation, and foot its own bills, or be taxed as a partnership (or a sole proprietorship which is, after all, simply a one-person partnership), and pass the income along to the owner or owners who then declare the profits as part of his, her, or their taxable income? Well, said the Court, in the *Kintner* case, a famous decision, there are four key little tests, and an entity is going to be taxed as a corporation unless it passes at least two of the tests by showing that in that regard, the entity isn't like a corporation. The four tests are easily described. They are: (1) free transferability of interest; (2) continuity of life; (3) limited liability; and (4) centralization of control. In each case, a "yes" answer is a point in favor of corporation; a "no" answer is one of not-a-corporation. Isn't that clear and simple? Of course not. Sometimes the answer to the question of the applicability of one or more of these tests to a specific situation can get unbelievably complex. And if you thought for a moment that the situation would be anything other than this continued confusion, then you may consider yourself to have been sentenced to go back and reread the five preceding chapters, and to stay after class for an attitude adjustment session.

Let's apply the tests to the LLC. We want to be taxed as a partnership, so we want to negate at least two of the four criteria. First, we recognize immediately that to prevail we're going to need to negate two issues out of issues (1), (2), and (4), because we must provide a positive answer for number three, the limited liability. If there's any one thing that a Limited Liability Company needs to provide to its members, it's limited liability.

In a recent spate of rulings, IRS has indicated that the restrictions on transferability of interests, the provisions for automatic dissolution if certain things happen, and the manager-versus-member control alternatives, can come together to provide that in three of the four test areas the LLC is more like a partnership than it is like a corporation, and so the LLC reports income for tax purposes as though it were a partnership. Please note well that what Internal Revenue has said is not that an LLC invariably *will* be treated as a partnership; IRS says only that the LLC *can* qualify to be treated as partnership.

A new development in this area is the 1996 announcement of "Check-the-Box" regulations. When finally adopted, these regulations will facilitate the efforts of an LLC to be taxed in the way it wishes. The four-pronged test described above will probably be reduced in importance, or maybe obviated altogether. To some extent, however, the general principles will continue to apply.

As with virtually all types of business entities, there are already developing some highly sophisticated variations on the simple theme, such as the use of American LLC's for foreign investors, the use of foreign corporations as managers of American LLC's, and the like. This is not the forum for a discussion of the concepts involved in that type of company. It is for us here only to point out one phenomenon: the most convoluted of these interlocking structures make much better cocktail party talk than they do investment vehicles.

What can we forecast at this time in history about the LLC? While it does not have the strict limit that the

Subchapter S corporation has on the number of members (or shareholders) or the strict limit that the Subchapter S corporation has on who can own a piece of it, the restrictions on assignability of interests applicable in most cases will probably serve to keep most LLC's fairly small and intimate structures. They won't become the new General Motors or IBM.

On the other hand, assuming the orderly growth of court opinions which provide guidelines for creating and operating LLC's, and assuming the continued development of a sufficient body of IRS rulings to permit the accountant and the attorney to find answers to the question that the perceptive client, like you, raises, we should be seeing a substantial number of LLC's formed to take their places in the family of business organizations. Certainly, they will be there owning commercial real estate and renting it for investment groups. One can be a member of an LLC and actively involved in its affairs without affecting his own personal exposure; in a limited partnership, on the other hand, a limited partner who takes an active role in running the show risks a court ruling that he was so active he became a general partner rather than a limited partner and, therefore, has personal liability. The ability of the LLC to have a trust of any type as a member opens the door to a potentially broad new range of family business units where the ownership gradually passes to the youngsters while the decision making rests in the gray heads who persist in thinking that age always means wisdom.

Suffice it for us here to urge you that if there will be at least two of you forming that new business which you have in mind, you need to at least consider the LLC as the structure of choice.

Playing for the Franchise

In our changing language, we have developed a new use for an old and well recognized word. The word is "franchise." It used to apply strictly to a form of special permission granted by a governmental agency for a specific type of activity. A selected Company (frequently, and totally coincidentally, headed by a major contributor to the most recent political campaign) would be granted the sole and exclusive right to collect garbage in the city or to provide electrical service or telephone service or the like. That Company would be said to "hold the franchise."

Usually, the type of service involved was one that needed to be done on an exclusive basis, because of the nature of the service. It would not be seemly, for example, to have several competing electric companies stringing wires down the same street, each one placing its own line of poles, installing its own set of transformers, and so on. So, one outfit would be selected and awarded the franchise, usually for a specific term of years. The rights and obligations of both the franchisor (the city) and the franchisee (the electric company) were negotiated elements of, and usually clearly spelled out in, the franchise contract.

It was not a change of law, but only a development in language that came to pass in the years following World War II, which brought a new meaning to the term. The concept had long been there and, in some industries, in use. Gasoline stations bearing the same name, the same general design, and, presumably selling the same products, existed all over the country. They were all, for example, Standard Oil stations, but each had a different owner. They were tied together purely by contract with the "Mother" company, Standard Oil. Their owner had acquired the right (and the obligation) to show the sign and logo of, to sell the products of, and to represent that he was a part of, Standard Oil.

The basic idea was that, as you drove from one city to another, you were more likely to drive into a service station whose name and products were familiar to you than one which was not. You knew and liked what you bought from Good Old Charlie at the Standard Oil station down the street from home, and so you expected, consciously or unconsciously, to get the same service, the same products, and the same advice from the Standard Station in Ogalalla, Nebraska, even though you had never met the people who operated it. From the standpoint of Sam, the service station operator in Ogalalla, there were enough persons driving through town, like you, who were accustomed to dealing with Charlie's Standard station in Pineville, or Mike's Standard Oil in Charleston, or something similar elsewhere, that there was a definite and positive value to Sam in hooking up with Standard Oil. So he contacted the Rockefeller folks in New York and told them he'd like to become a dealer for Standard Oil. From the standpoint of Standard Oil, of course, this was a situation with a lot going for it. It gave them captive distribution locations, with no investment. At the same time, it gave Sam a built-in customer base before he ever opened his business. But that, of course, is not the whole story.

Let's look, therefore, at the entire situation from a couple of steps further back, so that we can see the broader picture. A manufacturer, or a major distributor or service company, has a line of products or concepts which he would like to offer exclusively through stores which sell his product and his product only or, at least, primarily. Whether the product is gasoline or hamburgers, some of the problems that the Company faces are the same. The Company is aware that its reputation is based not only on the quality of the product which it produces and offers for sale, but upon the overall experience which the customer has when he goes into the store to purchase the product. If it's a service station we're concerned with, the cleanliness of the restroom may be as important as the cleanliness of the gasoline being pumped. The courtesy and helpfulness of the service (or the lack thereof) have a great deal to do with whether the traveler will seek out a station with the same sign in the next town and, therefore, these functions are matters of significance to the manufacturer. The neatness of the entire area is important. Certainly, the uniformity of signage is meaningful. When the manufacturer wants to run a nationwide sale, or a special on lube jobs, or whatever, he needs to know that the dealers who "fly his flag" will cooperate.

Other considerations may be even more important. Perhaps I buy Standard gasoline because I think their prices are, by and large, beneficial to me. So, the Standard

Oil Company wants to keep me happy with their pricing. Does that mean, therefore, that they have the right to tell good old Charlie how much he can charge for the gasoline he is selling me? Can they also tell good old Charlie what to wear to work? After all, we customers are used to seeing our service station attendants dressed in blue coveralls, and maybe seeing Charlie in his Hard Rock Cafe tee-shirt will injure the image. (Later, we'll have some more discussion about that Hard Rock Cafe tee-shirt, which gives rise to a whole bunch of different questions in the franchise area.) Surely, it's also important what days and what hours the service station is open, and what else they sell besides Standard Oil Products. Cigarettes? Slices of pizza? Soft drinks? State lottery tickets? How about racing forms, if the station is near the track? How about a religious book display? It can get hairy, indeed.

The central factor, however, is the risk that Standard Oil Company or whoever (let's start calling him by his right name, at least as far as this discussion goes, the Franchisor), takes upon granting to any contracting party the right to be one of his dealers. In some cases, there is a degree of intrinsic uniqueness to a product, but in most cases, the uniqueness is less important than, or is perhaps only one of the composite factors of, the franchisor's image. Maybe, the franchisor's gasoline, because it contains JX42, is better, and will make your car last years longer, or drive more safely or whatever. But I'll bet not. I'll bet that your car has lots of trouble distinguishing between X's gasoline, with the JX42, and Y's gasoline, which has added scridge in every drop, but no JX42.

So, the question is one of control. How much hegemony can the Franchisor exercise over his Franchisees, in the interest of offering consistency to his customers? There are several answers to offer, but before we get to that, let's note an important factor.

The uniformity which the franchisor seeks is not necessarily a uniformity of outward image. It may be something a great deal more subtle than that. I am aware of one "chain" of businesses which takes particular pride in the fact that there are no visible similarities of any nature between any two of the outlets which belong to the group. There is, however, a uniformity of systems practiced which produces uniformly acceptable output at all levels. The control exists.

Now, let's look at the same issues from Charlie's standpoint. "You're telling me," Charlie says, "that I'm going to invest my own money in real estate and install underground tanks and put in a three-bay service area with lifts and air compressors and all kinds of tools and go into hock up to my eyeballs, and then some clown from New-goddam-York is gonna tell me when to open and what to charge and what to wear and what else I can sell and all that? If I wanna work for somebody else, I'll read the Sunday paper want ads, fella." Well, hang in there, Charlie. Here comes the law to the rescue. Sorta. In part. Maybe.

Franchising today has become the one most striking characteristic of our contemporary business community. According to the International Franchise Association, there are over half a million franchised businesses in operation in the United States today. Thousands of new businesses open every month carrying one franchise flag or another. And, it appears, failure rates of businesses which are franchisees are notably lower than rates for non-franchised businesses.

In looking at the franchise field generally, we would be well advised to break it down into several groupings of franchises, according to business type, and then note the similarities and the differences. Let's also take note of the contractual distributorship relationship, which, for these purposes, is an entirely different breed of animal.

The locally owned and operated electronics store may be, by contract, the exclusive retail outlet in the community for Zilch stereo speaker systems. The store has a contract with Zilch International under which the store agrees to purchase eighty thousand dollars a year worth of speaker systems, and agrees to spend at least two hundred dollars a month on advertising them. In return, Zilch agrees that the store will be the only outlet in town for the product. The store sets its own prices, advertises as it sees fit, and gets nothing by way of direction from Zilch except perhaps an occasional suggestion for selling, and maybe a modest dollar contribution toward advertising costs. For this discussion, that's not a franchise. Not even if the store's sign says "Your only shop for Zilch Speakers."

There is a substantial difference between the Zilch store, on the one hand, and the Total Product Franchise, on the other hand, which is perhaps the most "captive" of all types of franchises. Let's assume that you have decided to open a greeting card store. You enter into an agreement with Footprint Greeting Cards, and the agreement provides (among other things) that:

1. You pay an opening franchise fee of $30,000;
2. You will have an opening capital investment of $20,000 in unencumbered cash;
3. You will lease a store of a size and at a location which the franchisor approves;
4. You will sell Footprint approved products and absolutely nothing else;
5. Your store will be open from 10 o'clock until 6 o'clock every day;
6. You will follow the pricing schedule and the sale schedule that you receive from week to week;

7. All employees, including you, will wear light tan skirts or slacks and light blue shirts;

8. All employees will attend a Footprint Smiling School before starting to work in the store;

9. You will send in, each week, a full report of sales and other activities on the form prepared and sent out by the Company;

10. And, you will pay to Footprint 4% of your gross sales each month for their help, in addition to buying everything you sell from them, at their prices and on their terms.

Before we reject, out of hand, a franchise of the nature just described, however, let's examine it a bit more thoroughly. No, it's not made for the free spirit, the entrepreneur who takes pride in marching to the beat of his own drummer, who creates for himself a business as a form of self expression. There is in our town a little store called "The Opinionated Bookseller," and it's owned, I am told, by a man who, repeatedly, will sell only those books he likes. I admire him. May his tribe increase. His is the spirit upon which our democracy is founded. But he ain't the norm. And he ain't the guy to sign a franchise agreement.

Franchises of the type described above for Footprint Greeting Cards didn't get that way because the founder of the company has an uncontrollably strong sphincter muscle, or because he wanted to be a Nazi but was born too late. The rigid rules grew out of a determination made that these principles, if followed, will enhance the chances for success sufficiently to make it worthwhile to spell them out and insist on them and check to see that they are being followed, and to employ contractual sanctions if they are disregarded. From the standpoint of the

Franchisee (that's you), rules of this nature will, in all likelihood, increase your chances of success in your effort. So perhaps you need to learn to live with them. Or, if you find them insufferable, maybe you need to find some other business or some other franchise.

Analogous to, and not very different from the Total Product Franchise is a business of the type that we can refer to as the Mostly Product Franchise. Here, the classic example is the fast food operation. This, perhaps more than any other area, is the type of business which changed the face of the nation over the past generation. There are those of us who remember a quaint early American custom, under which, if a restaurant was named Hudson's, that was because it was owned by Mr. and Mrs. Hudson. That also meant that if you dropped in for dinner one night you would be greeted by Mr. Hudson, who very sincerely expressed the hope that you would enjoy your meal. He wanted you to enjoy it, because if you did, you would come back and eat there again, and that was the way that Mr. and Mrs. Hudson earned a living and sent their kids to school or whatever. If you really wanted ketchup on your chateaubriand, Mr. Hudson brought it to you himself, in a little white dish. It was a very nice one-on-one situation, and there is some nostalgia and some sadness in its gradual disappearance from the scene.

Today, things are somewhat different. Compare the neighborhood McDonald's to Hudson's Restaurant. I don't know if there ever was a Mr. McDonald, or if there is one now. I sorta doubt it. I do know for sure that Mr. McDonald doesn't really know when I come in for a hamburger, nor does he particularly care whether I enjoy it or not, unless I'm part of a focus group upon which a statistical evaluation of the inner yearnings of the great masses of humanity is determined.

Nonetheless, and whatever, the huge numerical majority of purveyors of food ready to eat in these United States consists of food franchises, and the greatest number of these are so-called fast food operators. Most of them are no less demanding than the hypothetical greeting card company that we just discussed, and, for the most part, their insistences are much greater. For example, not only are you, the Franchisee, the operator, the person whose money is on the line, much more rigidly controlled as to appearance of the store, and hours of operation, and costumery of your staff and the like, you are also equally tightly controlled as to the entirety of your product line and the total recipe for each of the products which make it up. Imagine what would have befallen the KFC Franchisee who advertised that he used seven or eight of the Colonel's secret herbs and spices, but he threw out the others and substituted some basil and just a little tarragon. You are just as concerned with your customer's satisfaction as were Mr. and Mrs. Hudson, but there is little you can change to bring it about.

The voice of the Franchisor, which is, after all the voice of profitability, must have, and, by the language of the contract does have, total control over the real life-and-death matters like the exact weight of a hamburger, the exact content of the meat, the exact composition and flavor of the cheese, the structure of the deep-frying basket in which the french fries are made, and the like. It is frequently not essential that you purchase your raw materials (such as meat and buns) from the Franchisor, but there will normally be a Franchisor-approved supplier, and if you decide not to buy from him, the burden will be upon you to establish to the satisfaction of the Franchisor that the quality of the stir sticks supplied by your brother-in-law is equal in nature to that of the stir sticks supplied by the Franchisor's wife's cousin.

Next, let's look at the Primarily Service type of franchise. Here, we might be considering business such as while-u-wait car lubrication, the package wrap and ship store, or the party supply rental business. By and large, these are businesses in which the Franchisor seeks far less by way of control of the operation of the franchisee, because it is of less importance to the franchisor whether one specific franchisee does well, since there is less of a carryover from the reputation of one to the reputation of the others.

The last group of franchises is a relative late comer on the scene, but one which has been making up for lost time by rapid growth since the early eighties. These are the Service Only Franchises. They can be divided into two groups for our consideration, those which promote a product, but a product in which they have no individuality, and those that offer no product at all.

An example of the former group is the travel agency. Their products are airline tickets and auto rentals and cruise arrangements and hotel reservations and the like. There is nothing distinctive in any way about what they offer. A ticket on United Airlines Flight 250 to Anchorage purchased through one travel agency is not distinguishable from a ticket on the same flight bought through another agency or bought directly from the airline itself. Usually, there is no difference in price. And actually, there is no difference in quality or function.

The other type of company inhabiting this classification is the operation that has no product at all, but offers just a straight service. Examples of this type of business are the real estate agency and the income tax preparation office. Like dealing with the travel agency, it makes no difference in the product if I buy my house through Nationwide Housesellers, or the one-man office of Seymour Holmes, Realtor, or even if I buy it directly from the last owner of the house, without professional intervention. Yet, there has been a huge growth in franchises of businesses like travel agencies and tax preparers in the last ten years, and, therefore, one assumes that there must be a valid reason for the phenomenon. There is. Or rather, there are. And it is the existence of these reasons that gives rise to a significant difference in the franchisor-franchisee relationships here, compared to such relationships in the fast food and scented soap stores.

In both cases, the travel agency and the real estate agency, the Franchisor must concern himself greatly with image, and with continuity from office to office, because that's the only way he has to distinguish his operations from those of his competitor. So, the franchisor must demand that his franchisee use nothing but blue and white striped signs, and that all employees wear little green ties, and so on. And he wants to be sure that all the offices use the same letterhead and the same cards and brochures and such. Beyond that, his efforts at showing identity become difficult. He has no product, as such, and no label.

An even stronger demonstration of the point can be seen in hotels and motels, which also fit into the category. For example, while all Holiday Inns are not architecturally identical, Holiday Inn has used as an advertising program the suggestion that the traveler wants to stay in places where there are no surprises, i.e., where the service rendered is the same in one place as in another.

The nature of the business dictates, therefore, that while the Franchisor may see less of a need to assure himself of the desirability of the location from which you have chosen to operate, and he has a lesser concern about your continued solvency, since you are not buying all your inventory from him, he needs to offer far more assistance in, and far more hegemony over, the performance of services by your personnel. So, his franchise agreement is more deeply concerned with training, with standards of staffing, with outward appearances of your office, and with nature, level, and speed of service that you offer than with your ability to buy goods.

Whatever the type of franchise, it should be beyond question that you need to exercise extreme caution before signing the franchise agreement. If the situation permits, it would be prudent to compare the franchise contract you are offered with contracts offered by other franchisors in the same type of business. You will find variances in the franchise fee, the ongoing service fees, the advertising contributions, the services to be rendered, the availability of assistance, and the performance requirements imposed on you.

Fortunately for you, the potential franchisee, there are some significant legal safeguards which have been erected for your protection, and your assistance. Most states have offices called the Department of Business Opportunities, or something of the like. The office is analogous to the Securities Department or Division, with its role in the offering of stocks. That is, the law of most jurisdictions provides that a Franchisor may offer his program in that state only if his corporation has qualified to do business in that state and appointed an agent to accept process (i.e., to receive the papers if he is sued), and if he has submitted for approval an offering circular explaining in some detail what the Franchisor is, what the franchise is, what his track record is, and so forth. In addition, the Federal Trades Commission has entered the lists to some extent, but not nearly in the way that the Securities and Exchange Commission has stepped into the field of stock sales.

There is a Uniform Franchise Offering Circular which has been designed and which has been prescribed as the controlling device in a majority of the states, and, in those states, no franchise can be sold without the purchaser having received copies of the UFOC (here we are with the acronyms again, but this time please be very careful with your pronunciation) and given a sufficient opportunity to read and evaluate it. No UFOC's can be given out until the state has approved them. Like the stock prospectus, when a governmental office has given its blessing to the offering circular, remember, nobody has said that this is a good deal. Nobody has even said that what is reported on the circular is all true. The state has merely acknowledged that the Franchisor has discussed with sufficient thoroughness each of the subjects which he is required by statute or regulation to discuss in the offering circular.

For example, there is almost always a requirement that the circular specify the names and addresses of the persons who control the Franchisor corporation, and tell what each of them has been doing for the last five years. If the circular tells you that the President of the Franchisor has been running a television network and a steel processing plant and a chain of restaurants while serving as Governor of Idaho, nobody in the State Capital bothered to look any of it up and see if maybe he has in fact been working as a janitor in Filene's Basement. The check is only to see if the Franchisor has answered the question of what has this guy been doing for the last five years.

Some states require the circular to tell you how many franchises have opened up and how many have gone broke, and that's helpful information. They're also required to give you the names and numbers of other franchisees, so that you can talk with them, and that helps too. Most important, of course, is the requirement that you be advised as to the essential provisions of the franchise agreement. That, of course, is the most important information of all, and it is that with which you should become familiar before you do your decision making.

What are the important legal considerations about all of this? What are the controlling rules about franchises that you need to have in front of you when you decide whether to go the franchise route?

First, as noted above, you need to find out what your state has as a Franchise, or Business Opportunity, law, because in this area, the range of degrees of state coverage is huge. In some states, such as Montana, there is no statute at all, no regulations and no controls. The federal law, the interest of the Federal Trade Commission, is all that there is. Wisconsin, on the other hand, is a true mother to its citizens. It requires the most comprehensive of offering circulars, and it will accept a filing only from a franchisor which has satisfied some rigorous requirements to prove its own viability, and its persistence in getting the authorities of the state to respond at all.

Armed with the knowledge of the scope of protection that your state offers, you ask for and receive the packet of information that the Franchisor has prepared. It's up to you to do your "due diligence" with it. Probably the one most useful and helpful action that you can take is to visit in person several of the other franchisees in the region. If they are happy with the Franchisor, chances are strong that they will be willing to meet with you, and to discuss the prospects. If they are unwilling to discuss the situation with you at all, that too might tell you something.

Other information contained in the offering circular will be self-explanatory to some extent, but if the pamphlet is sending signals that you're not receiving, this is not time to stand on ceremony. If you're not sure what the balance sheet and profit and loss statements are saying, you owe it to yourself (and, probably to your creditors as well) to find a friendly accountant who will make himself or herself available to translate the numbers into information. Other professionals can comment to you on the other aspects of the circular.

Next, there is the body of law which has grown up in the field, setting the outer limits on what the parties to the franchise agreement can do, and describing what happens if they go beyond those parameters. For example, a franchisor can agree with you that you will be his only franchisee in a designated geographic area, and you will have the right to sue him if he licenses someone else to open up across the street from you. But he cannot prevent the franchisee in the next town from selling to the folks in your neighborhood.

Similarly, as you may remember from the big Chrysler Corporation ruckus a few years ago, there has emerged from our court system a concept of the proprietary right of the franchisee. That is, once you have invested money and time and effort in building up your business as a franchisee, there are limitations upon the authority of the Franchisor to "cut you off at the pass." On the other hand, when you enter into a franchise agreement you commit yourself to be bound, to a greater or lesser extent, depending on the nature of the business and the particular Franchisor's document, to certain specified patterns of behavior. By and large, it would serve you well to adhere to these rules. Remember, in most cases, the Franchisor is a lot bigger than you, is a lot better equipped than you are to fight out the question in the courts, and can pick and choose the arena to fight in.

The question of what business form to pursue if you're going to be a franchisee is not significantly affected by the terms of the franchise, but there is an additional fact to note. Most franchisees will choose to operate as corporations, in order to have the protection of limited liability that the corporate form permits. The franchisor, on the other hand, will frequently insist upon granting the franchise to the individual, or, at least, to requiring the principals of the franchisee corporation to guarantee personally all the obligations which the franchisee undertakes by signing the franchise agreement.

To offset the frightening aspects of the franchise relationship, there are two large and meaningful advantages which stand out, and which, in a properly run operation, will offset many times over the fees involved. Let's look at them. But first, let's look at what those fees are. As a general rule, there is an opening franchise fee, which may range from a low of a few thousand dollars to fifty thousand dollars or more in some cases. This is a one-time payment, and it may be based to some extent on the size and expectation of the operation. The other charge is the ongoing monthly (or weekly) service charge, which is normally calculated as a percentage of gross sales. The percentage will vary, depending on the industry, and the nature of the operation, and, wonder of wonders, what the traffic will bear. Two to six percent of sales is a normal range for the small-ticket item seller, except, of course, for the business where you buy all your merchandise from the Franchisor, and there, he can put his share into the cost of the inventory that you buy from him.

Here's the payback. As for the opening franchise fee, let's admit that virtually every new business loses money for its first period of operation—maybe six months, perhaps up to two years. If there is any way that the learning period required to get to a black bottom line can be shortened, that route should be sought out and eagerly embraced. Now, the reason that the franchisor is there is that he knows a great deal more about operating this type of business than you do, and what he is selling, among other things, is the right to profit from his knowledge. If his advice as to location saves you from a dead end, you have saved a bundle. Advice as to opening inventory, as to staffing, and a dozen other matters are translatable into immediate savings.

Next, by opening as a franchisee, you have, from day one, a name which has already acquired a recognition factor. It attracted you, didn't it? For a thousand reasons, the gross sales on the first day of operation of a new Baskin & Robbins store can be expected to be somewhat larger than the sales on day one at Franny & Zooey's ice cream concoctions.

In addition to the enhanced value at opening, there are areas of ongoing value which the franchisee receives, and which support the payment of ongoing service fees, which fees can amount to significant sums. First, the franchisor can and often does act as a supplier in ways other than as a distributor of the primary merchandise which you sell to the public. Often, those items can be supplied at substantially lower costs than you would have to pay as an individual contracting party. Bags, stickers, electric signs, employee uniforms, napkins, brochures, labels, all come a lot cheaper when produced by the thousands. Advertising, when purchased cooperatively by a large group of businesses, can be much cheaper than when individually tailored. And so it goes.

Many franchisors offer their franchisee the ongoing opportunity to send their new employees to training programs, the value of which can far exceed the cost to the franchisee. The graduate becomes much more quickly a valuable addition to the franchisee's team. Granted, in some cases the cost to the franchisee is excessive and in some cases the training is of very little value. But that's part of the evaluating you did when you did your due diligence and decided which franchisor to sign up with.

Case law—the body of laws that we call the "common law"—is still developing as courts find themselves dealing more and more frequently with the whole area of franchisees. With respect to the issuance of the franchise in the beginning, we know that in virtually every case, you, the potential franchisee, are protected by both Federal and State law, designed to assure you that you are given sufficient information upon which to base your decision of affiliation, telling you whether a given franchise opportunity is a good one or a bad one, a money maker or a loser. We know, next, that the franchise contract, the agreement that you sign when you buy the right to operate the franchise, spells out with considerable specificity and clarity what you can expect and demand from the franchisor, and what he can expect and demand from you.

Next, we know that entering into a franchise can be, and usually is, the beginning of a long and intimate relationship between two very unequal parties, and the franchisee is the lesser of the two. Controversies can and do and will arise between a franchisee and a franchisor. When they do, let's admit it, you as the franchisee can find yourself at a considerable disadvantage. You are dealing with a contract prepared, usually exclusively or almost exclusively, by the franchisor's attorney. Usually, the franchisor can afford the battle more easily than you. The franchisor has more money, more power, more clout, and more knowledge than you do. Your relationship is like that of the pig and the chicken who were discussing the value of ham and eggs. As the pig said to the chicken, "To you it's a modest contribution; to me its total commitment." When you enter into a franchise, as the franchisee, to you, in most cases, it's total commitment.

Further, in some cases, there are specialized statutes dealing with the business. For example, a Federal law, the Petroleum Marketing Practices Act, sets out some of the rules governing wholesale and retail distribution of gasoline. Originally, the statute appeared necessary because the Congress recognized that it might be desirable to level the playing field for dealings between the major oil distributors (like Exxon, or Texaco) and the man-and-wife team who want to open a service station right out there where you get off the interstate to come into town. Seemed a good idea. The early proceedings contained testimony about things such as "contracts of adhesion." (A contract of adhesion is where the big guy says to the little guy, "Here's the deal. Take it or leave it. Sign it the way we printed it or go away.") It's hard to describe this kind of contract as freely negotiated, hammered out between men of good will with a sense of fairness and compromise. Somehow, with the new law, a funny thing happened on the way to the law books. Lots of large well-informed providers of information made presentations to the Congressional Committee and to the drafters of the new act. Now, the doors to the committee rooms were equally open to the major oil companies and to the little guy with the corner service station and most congressmen were just as willing to hear from and meet with the little guy as the major campaign contributors. Somehow, however, the law that finally came out seemed to many to do very little to level the playing field; some would even suggest that it ended up increasing the tilt.

Whether the Petroleum Marketing Practices Act increased or decreased the equality of the parties is a matter about which reasonable men may differ. It is interesting to note, however, that of the reported cases tried in the federal courts under the act, the major oil companies are batting better than .950.

At any rate, even with the statutes like the Petroleum Marketing Practices Act, the point remains the same. The information is available. The rules of the game are there for you to see and think about. The choice is yours. If a franchise chain has been in business for some years, it must be because it has some well-satisfied and successful franchisees. The franchisees are there for you to visit and meet with and talk to. (If they are not, that tells you something, doesn't it?) The field opens thousands of opportunities for you to consider. Make a free, wise, well thought through, uncontrolled decision.

A few final observations about franchises: the franchisor can promise you that he won't open up any other franchises in your "protected area" but he can't—nor can you—prevent another of his franchisees from selling "your" customers. The franchisor can give you only as much exclusivity as the anti-trust laws and the general rules of business permit.

Similarly, your franchisor is honor-bound—and contract bound—to assist you and help you and protect you from encroachment by others; but he is equally bound and determined to protect his other franchisees against you.

Last, you may well find in your franchise agreement a provision limiting your ability to compete for a two-year or longer period if and when you and the franchisor come to a parting of the ways. Like other contractual provisions, it's a two-way street. If the activity prohibited is reasonable, and the geographic restriction is reasonable, and the time restriction is reasonable, the prohibition is enforceable. That's a part of the contract you agreed to.

Finally, be aware that you are entering a relationship with a large Company (compared to you), represented by its own staff of attorneys and accountants. The wisest expenditure of dollars that you can make is to seek out, use, talk with, and listen to your advisors. Their training and their experience equip them to point out problems, and gaps, and nuances of meaning that you could be overlooking. Your enthusiasm could well be such that you are overlooking points that you would ordinarily notice.

Further, your attorney can, in most cases, negotiate some variations in the franchise contract that will be of substantial benefit to you. It doesn't matter that the contract is already printed, on thick paper with important gew-gaws across the top. Even printed contracts can be changed before they are signed. The franchisor is as eager to close the deal as you are; after all, that's the business he is in, selling franchises. And right now, you're the customer. Have a little spunk. Then sign up, and become the best franchise in the system.

7

What Else Do I Need to Know?

OTHER VARIATIONS ON THE THEME

While the preceding chapters have given you a very brief overview of the different types of business entities available for you to choose among, one cannot overemphasize the fact that the list is not exclusive, and the portrait gallery contains pictures of only the most prominent members of the family, not all.

One type of business entity not discussed in detail here, for example, is the business trust. In Kentucky these are provided for by statute. The business trust, which is a device most frequently used for the ownership and maintenance of real estate, may be established for essentially any business purpose where the business consists of owning and dealing in income-producing property. This would apply whether we are considering real estate or stock or mortgages or other property of a similar nature. The trustees, who may number one or many, according to the document which establishes the trust, own the title to the property put into the trust, and handle it for the benefit for the beneficiaries of the trust, in whatever way the trust document requires. The trust issues certificates of beneficial ownership, which certificates look for all the world like stock certificates. They can be sold and transferred in the same manner as stock, and their sale and transfer can be limited in the same manner as can stock certificates.

The business trust comes into being when the document, entitled a "declaration of trust," is filed with the Secretary of State, at the capital, and, generally, when a copy is also filed in the county in which the trust does business. The beneficiaries of the trust, who are not necessarily the persons who set the trust up, but are the persons declared by the trust documents to be the beneficiaries, are taxed on their distributable share of the income in the same way as though they were partners in a partnership. The beneficiaries are not personally liable for the debts of the trust, beyond the extent of their shares of the trust property itself.

Another new variation on an old theme was created by the same statute that authorized the LLC. This is the Registered Limited Liability Partnership, which is essentially a variation upon the limited partnership arrangement described elsewhere in this discussion.

Sometimes, businesses are engaged in by the Estate of a Decedent, although usually this is just a temporary situation, continuing only while the affairs of the deceased owner of the business are being put in order.

Other maverick forms of business entities come into being, from time to time, as do strange and unusual combinations of common forms of business. As we have noted earlier in this discussion, partnerships can be the stockholders in corporations, and corporations can be the stockholders in corporations. Corporations can be partners in a partnership, and partnerships can be partners in a partnership. A trust can be a partner and a trust can be a stockholder. The combinations, and the nuances of combination, are virtually endless. The field is ever fertile for the imaginative constructor, and it is full of land mines for the unwary investor. For example, we have not discussed (and we are not going to discuss) options, futures, calls and puts, rights of first refusal, or a thousand and one other variations on the basic theme. First, there are already more than enough works available on the subject, ranging from the scholarly to the unscrupulous (and sometimes a combination thereof). Second, our discussion here is limited to a very basic view of "how shall I set my business up?"

BUYING AN EXISTING BUSINESS

Throughout our brief journey, we have looked into the matter of establishment of a new business. Perhaps, therefore, before completing our conversation, we should look briefly into the subject of the purchase of a going business. Virtually every comment contained in these pages is equally applicable to the purchase of a business, although, in some instances, the decisions that we have described as needing to be made, have already been made for you. On the other hand, if the business in question is worth being purchased, buying it rather than creating it is probably a more expensive route to travel. While the entire scope of such a transaction is not within the area that this book is talking about, a few things need to be noted. First, an acquisition takes one of two forms. Either it is the purchase of a collection of assets that constitute a going business, or it is the purchase of shares of stock in a corporation which corporation, in turn, owns the business being bought. In either case, there are all kinds of questions that need to be answered, all kinds of assurances that you need to receive, and, above all, all kinds of backups that you need to the promises and assurances, the warranties and representations, that come along with the package. A promise, remember, is only as good as the promisor. A written and sealed and notarized assurance that you are getting good and clear and clean title to everything you are purchasing is not very helpful if the seller is insolvent and unreliable. You need to know that what you are buying can be transferred freely and clearly and totally. A lease to the most desirable location in town has value, but if you need the landlord's consent to take it over from the old tenant, that lease is not a very valuable item until the landlord has given that consent. Your seller may have a trade name with all the pizzazz and romance in the world, but if he doesn't have the ownership right to transfer it, its value to you is not very significant. The inventory may be clean and salable, but if the bank has a first mortgage on it, you could end up paying for it twice.

Similar questions can arise when you are purchasing the stock of a corporation that is already in business. Under these circumstances, the owner of the business doesn't change. The corporation owns the business before you bought it, and it owns the business after you bought it. The only difference is in who owns the stock of the corporation. In that case, you need all the information described above and, then, there are additional things that you need to know. You need to know also that when you have bought the stock that the seller has laid on the table, you will have effective control of the corporation. You need to know that there isn't someone else lurking in the next room who has an option to acquire several thousand additional shares of stock from the corporation. You need to know that the stock that you are agreeing to buy isn't subject to a right of first refusal held by somebody else.

The purchase of a going business, in short, is complex, is technical, and has built-in risks. That's why the woods are full of professionals: attorneys, accountants, business brokers, and appraisers. While you may not need the entire selection for one transaction, and while you may be able to have complete and justified trust and confidence in all the persons you are dealing with, the dollars that you spend assembling your professional team may well prove to be the best bargain of the entire deal. You should trust your mother, as the saying goes, but you should still cut the cards.

What does this whole mass of leeches do to earn their keep? What makes them worth while? Here's what. There are ways of assuring yourself of the Seller's ability to deliver good and clean title to you. Deeds and titles and mortgages and security agreements and liens are all of record in the courthouse, available to be checked. Sampling and auditing provide reliable devices for checking accounts and lists. The Seller's own books of account, if he makes them available to you, can disclose all kinds of evaluation data to one who knows where to look. Trademarks, Patents, Trade Names, Designs, Copyrights—these can be and should be checked out in Washington via relatively inexpensive processes. All of this testing can and should be accomplished by the attorney and the accountant who are on your team. And they can, and should, provide you with written opinions.

Well, what if the Seller won't open up his books and records to you? In many cases, that tells you something and perhaps you would be well advised to listen well. In other situations there may be good reason for the hush-hush, but you know the risks, and you make a decision.

Is there anything further you can do to protect yourself? Of course, there is. First, you can demand guaranteed protection. If you are buying assets from a corporation controlled by one Seller, and you know that the selling corporation won't stay around long enough to stand behind its obligations, then you demand the personal guarantee and indemnification of the corporation's main stockholder or stockholders.

Where there isn't enough practical guaranty around anywhere to allow you to sleep at night, you "escrow the price." That is, if you're buying a business for $300,000 in cash, your contract provides that the Seller gets $200,000 at closing, and the remaining $100,000 is held back until enough time has elapsed to permit you to assure yourself that you did indeed get what you bought.

In many states, there is on the books a "Bulk Sales Law" which requires a notice to be sent to all the creditors of a business about to be purchased. The creditors have a short time in which to assert their claims against the assets or the selling price; when that time has passed, the Buyer knows that his assets are free of claims. (Of course, like many other laws referred to in the preceding pages, the parties generally use sworn statements and proof of payment to obviate all the notifying.) The point remains, however, and the value of the Bulk Sales Law is like that of other statutes: The fact that it is there produces desirable behavior that might not take place if the static inertia of the statute were not there to begin with.

Two other aspects of the acquisition of a going business should be recited briefly. First, there is what is usually the most valuable asset of all, and the real reason for buying an already established business. That is the cadre of employees who may come along with the package. They know the procedures and the products and the people and the pitfalls and the perils and the potential. (The "P" words?")

There are many cases in which one of the required elements of the deal is the entry into agreements which cause the key personnel to stay with the Company being purchased. Occasionally the requirement is imposed by the seller, out of concern for his loyal troops; most frequently, however, a thoughtful buyer sees that the employees are the most important aspect of the public image of the Company, as well as the central aspect of its efficiency. Such a buyer, therefore, establishes as a condition to his completion of the purchase, that certain key employees agree to stay on the team.

Let's pause here for a minute. We've just used a term that could be one of those weird words we spoke of in the very first pages—words that are perfectly common words in ordinary use, but which take on a different and very specific meaning when used in a business law context. Here, the word is "condition." So, let's stand back and get a broader view.

When a Seller and a Buyer come to a meeting of the minds and agree to the sale and purchase of a business (or of a house, or a horse, or whatever), the whole conversation and negotiation is distilled into one document, called an "Agreement" or a "Contract." As a general rule, except in cases of fraud or the like, all the conversation, all the tire-kicking and smell testing, all the boasting and puffery are condensed into the words in that document. If it's not written into the document, it doesn't matter if he said it or not.

This all-important piece of paper, the Agreement, or the Contract, contains (a) Undertakings, (b) Warranties and Representations, and (c) Conditions. An example of an Undertaking (sometimes called simply a "Term") is the Price: "Buyer promises to pay Seller One Hundred Thousand Dollars in cash at the closing." An Undertaking is something that one of the parties to the contract promises to do. It is part of the consideration. If a party fails to follow through and perform that which he has promised or undertaken, he has broken or "breached" the contract.

An example of a Warranty or Representation would be "Seller warrants that all of the Company's trucks are owned free and clear of any claims." If the parties were to gather at the closing table and the Buyer's attorney were to announce that in doing his checking he found that the Company still owed five hundred dollars on one of the trucks, the deal would not fail, but we would have a minor breach of a warranty, and the Seller would be obligated to pay off the note on the truck before the closing was completed. Very substantial breaches of warranty (like he's trying to sell a company he doesn't even own) have, of course, much greater consequences.

An example of a Condition would be a provision that Buyer's obligation to complete the purchase is conditioned upon his being able to secure a lease on the store premises from the landlord for at least five years at the same rent as Seller has been paying. If Buyer were to find, after signing the contract, that his efforts to persuade the landlord to give him a five-year lease were unsuccessful and the best the landlord would offer was two years, the condition would not have been met. Buyer, therefore, would have a choice. He could walk away from the deal and abort the purchase, with neither Seller nor Buyer having any liability to the other by reason of the failure. Or, if he wished, Buyer could "waive the condition" and agree to complete the transaction without the five-year lease.

It follows, of course, that where there is a good faith failure of a condition, Buyer and Seller could, if they both agreed, recast the contract and close on different terms:

"Well, Seller, without the five-year lease, it's not worth a hundred thousand, but I'll give you ninety-seven five."

"That's a deal. I'll get my lawyer to draft an amendment to the contract."

At any rate, when the warranties and representations are met and the conditions are satisfied (or waived) and the dust has settled, the closing takes place. Money changes hands and the Company has a new owner.

The use of the term "closing" prompts another trip off onto a slight tangent. "Closing" is another of those terms that lawyers tend to throw off in conversation without any consideration of whether the other parties to the conversation have or haven't an idea as to what the term refers to. So let's cure that defect.

In a manner of speaking, every transaction has a "closing." When I buy an ice cream cone, I hand the lady $1.10, and she hands me a chocolate chip cone. The passage of items from her hand to mine, and from my hand to hers constitute the closing. It is the completion of the contract. Using some of the terms we have just finished discussing, the conditions are over, although the warranties and representations may persist. Certainly she would have a legal right to complain if it turned out that the dollar bill I handed her was counterfeit, since I impliedly warranted that I was handing her real money. Equally certainly, I would have a right to complain, in a court if necessary, should it turn out that I got food poisoning from the ice cream cone. Other than that, however, the transaction is over. She has the money she sought, and I have the calories and fat grams that I couldn't live without.

In the world of higher finance, a closing may be (but doesn't have to be) a bit more formal. Whether we are speaking of the purchase of a home or the purchase of a business, there is frequently, but not always, a gathering of the entire cast of characters, usually in the office of either the Buyer's attorney or the Seller's attorney, or sometimes at a bank. They play the time-honored game of "I'll show you mine if you show me yours." The Seller produces whatever deeds, bills of sale, waivers, agreements of others, transfers of corporate stock, and other papers that the contract calls for. The Buyer produces money. When the Buyer's attorney has checked through all the paper work and pronounced it fit, or has rewritten the parts he didn't like, he lets it be known, and the Buyer hands over the bucks. As a practical matter, of course, the papers have generally been thoroughly negotiated out and checked days before in dealings between the attorneys, and there should be no surprises.

At the other end of the scale, a "closing" can be as simple as a delivery of papers between offices by attorneys, or by couriers or by mail, it being fairly clearly understood by all that if the piece of paper you give me (a check, for instance) turns out to be no good, you can tear up and throw away, or return to me, the transfer papers I gave you, since any court will invalidate them if I ask.

Generally, although not in every case, the right of possession transfers from Seller to Buyer at the same time as the right of ownership passes. In common parlance, the Seller gives the keys to the Buyer at the same time that he hands him the title. There are situations, however, where the two are not simultaneous, and different arrangements are required. For example, sometimes in transferring a business where there is a liquor license, there is a delay in the time when the Buyer can assert complete ownership of the business, because he cannot do so until the State has granted him the right to sell alcoholic beverages. So, the Buyer operates the business for a time as the theoretical "agent" of the Seller. In other words, he is running the business as an employee of the Seller until his own license comes through. Of course, the terms of the "employment" are that the employee keeps all the profits and pays all the bills, but the theory is that he is not really the owner. If, of course, the license fails to come through, the whole contract is backed out and canceled.

Often, there is another party present at the closing, and sometimes he is the most important person of all. This is the banker who is lending the Buyer some large portion of the purchase price. He and his professional henchmen will also be checking out matters such as clear title to assets and the like. At the closing, the Buyer will sign a promissory note to the bank in return for the purchase money dollars that the bank has brought to the table. That note will be secured, usually, by a security interest given on the business assets to the bank, involving two documents. These are a financing statement, which is a very brief announcement for all the world to read, stating that the XYZ National Bank has a security interest in all the business assets of the ABC hot dog stand, and a security agreement, which is your contract with the bank, spelling out the terms of your indentured servitude. Together, those two documents are to personal property what the mortgage is to real property.

At any rate, and in a very brief summary, the steps to buying an existing business are these: (1) negotiate, draft and sign a binding contract; (2) complete the due diligence of checking out everything that can be questioned; (3) satisfy the conditions; and (4) close the transaction. So, in a manner of speaking, the Buyer's opening comes right after his closing.

SELECTING YOUR PROFESSIONAL TEAM

Throughout this discussion, we've touched at various times on the desirability of representation by competent counsel throughout the dealings leading up to the day when you have your own business out there as a part of the economy. Let's dig into that one a little deeper. First, of course, let's note that there is no requirement that you be represented by anyone. It's not like being accused of murder, where the state will appoint an attorney to represent you if you don't have one of your own. It's also not a matter of everybody is out to get you and to rob you blind and to pull the wool over your eyes so you darn well better have your own sneaky Pete to slip one or two over on them because you gotta get them before they get you. Most of all, it's not a matter of hiring an expert to do your decision making for you, since if you're not prepared to do your own decision making, maybe you shouldn't be going into business at all. Okay, if all that is what it's not, then what is it? The transactional attorney today is a lawyer whose knowledge and experience qualify him to set out to you at length, and much more specifically than in these pages, the questions that you need to ask of yourself and others before you make the decision to take the plunge into your own business. And if he or she is comfortable and confident, you'll also be the beneficiary of statements with respect to some of the issues raised that, "I don't know the answer to that, but I know where you can go to find out, or I'll help you find out where to go to ask."

These questions can range from whether the property is properly zoned, to whether there are differences in taxation resulting from being on one side of the city limit's line or another, to what types of financing are available, to what licensing is needed and what it takes to get it, and so on and so on. And, of course, to what you need to ask to determine what form of business structure is probably your best choice.

Next, your attorney's experience as a negotiator should serve you in good stead. Negotiation is both an art and a science. There are techniques and ploys which are available to use and which, in the hands of a skilled practitioner, produce meaningful differences in the final results. Your attorney isn't negotiating *for* you, he is negotiating *with* you. Together you are a team, playing a game in which it is possible for all sides to come out as winners ... but also where it is possible for all sides to come out losers.

When the negotiating has reached the handshake stage, your attorney takes center stage and, for a while, he is working for you, not with you. He is drafting the contract documents, alone or in concert with the Seller's attorney. Again, it's not a matter of slipping one through, but nuances of wording can become very important should questions of interpretation subsequently arise.

After the documents are written and signed, you need guidance on what kinds of checking and arranging you should be doing. Here, your attorney will be determining the corporate health of your Seller, whether there are any liens against the assets you are buying, whether all taxes have been paid, and matters of that nature. Meanwhile, you are lining yourself up with suppliers, and the landlord and such. Together you and your attorney are negotiating and solidifying your financing arrangements.

It's at this stage that you are also setting up your business structure, your corporation, or partnership or LLC or whatever, and again it's your attorney's role to present the key questions, to help find the answers, and then to draft the needed papers, and put them in the proper places. At the same time, your attorney is preparing (together with the attorney for the Seller) the closing documents, the deeds, transfers of property, leases, and so on. He is also preparing the other documents you'll need right after closing, such as employment contracts for your key personnel and matters like that.

At the closing, your attorney is the master of ceremonies. Sometimes he plays this role jointly with the Seller's attorney, but it's your guy or gal who can usually assert the leading role, because he (or she) is the one holding the dollars, ready to deliver when the auguries are right. And you know the Golden Rule: he who has the gold makes the rules.

Well, that's a big job. How much should you pay for all that fooforall? As usual with the questions we've been looking into, there are no hard and fast answers. Although the latest trends are to get away from the habit, most transactional attorneys still charge by the hour. On the one hand, that seems fair, because expenses occur by the hour. You pay your employees by the hour, you pay your rent and your mortgage and your telephone bill by the month. On the other hand, first, you have no idea of how many hours your attorney actually put in on the job. Second, you have no way of knowing how essential those hours were. Did he charge you for two hours researching a point of law that he really should have known the answer to? If you pay him to research that question and he comes across the same question for another client next week, should that client reimburse you for half of your attorney's research time? On the other hand, this is an objective form of measure, and in the hands of an honest attorney, it is not something abused. (The attorney you hired is an *honest* one, right?)

Others will charge by the transaction, maybe a flat fee, or, more likely, a flat fee with all kinds of riders and exceptions. Here, there are other problems. This is a matter for negotiation between you. And who are you hiring? The best negotiator you can find, that's who. And that's great when he is negotiating for you. But when he is negotiating WITH you?

Although it is a situation fraught with conflicts, and almost never a desirable one, there are also those attorneys who offer to handle the matter in return for a share of the company, say 5 to 10 percent. There are probably some situations where that is a very fair arrangement, and certainly it is an aid to one who is somewhat undercapitalized anyway. It does have, however, two very compelling drawbacks. The first of these is that it ties you to that lawyer on a more or less permanent basis, and that just doesn't feel right. If the relationship works, nobody needs any artificial ties to keep it in place. Maybe he was the best in the world to help you get started, but not the attorney you'd pick to handle other problems that may arise down the road. And this is quite clear to you but not to him. Things have to get pretty sticky before you call a meeting of shareholders or partners or whatever and vote 90-to-10 to hire a lawyer who is a competitor of your 10 percent partner.

The other problem is one of arithmetic. When you're starting out with a business worth $25,000, giving the attorney a 10 percent interest in return for a $2,500 piece of work seems about right. But you do the job you expected of yourself all along, and ten years down the road that little $25,000 investment is worth a million and a half. Now that little $2,500 job is worth $150,000 to him, and you'll never get him out of there. Unintentionally, you are some of the seed corn.

Anyway, the important rule here is to have an understanding about fees at the beginning. If the attorney doesn't raise the question at the first meeting, then you raise the question. Matters of this nature are not like birthdays; surprises aren't nice.

All of this brings us to a most important question. How do you go about finding and hiring this attorney? Let's talk about that. The selection that you have before you today is, unfortunately for you and the attorneys as well, much too broad. The field of practicing attorneys is too large, and that breeds problems.

Time was when the study of law approached that of a calling. "The law is a cruel mistress and will brook no other love," as a sixteenth-century scholar of the English common law put it. The law student made a three-year commitment to total immersion, and he graduated with something of a sense of a role in promoting the welfare of the entire community. Of course, those were also the days when students went to medical school to learn to heal people.

Anyway, over the years that followed, the university found itself losing ground in the race for dollars needed to stay alive. Unlike other graduate schools, all that it took to increase revenue from the law school was to stick a few more chairs in the classroom. So the number of lawyers being spewed out into society more than doubled over a twenty-year span, and the demand for lawyers stayed at just about the same level. Further, the quality of the fledglings declined. What happened? Nothing good.

Today, also, the law has become far more complex than ever before. A more complex society not only requires a more complex legal system, it spawns one. Rapidly changing economics produce rapidly changing laws. Larger population masses require more regulation, and therefore more law. Becoming a world community requires more complex legal regulation. It's a jungle out there and the undergrowth is thickening.

The combined result of all this is that a surfeit of less well trained lawyers are competing, advertising, and sniping at each other in search of the right to do work for which many of them are unqualified. It is no wonder that there has been a proliferation of lawyer jokes.

So how do you pick and choose and employ? First, you recognize that there are today all sorts of lawyers, and you are looking for a specific genre. One who has acquired a splendid reputation for handling criminal matters or personal injury cases or divorces is not thereby automatically equally adept in the area where you seek assistance. He may be just as able in negotiating a lease as he is in swaying a jury on the subject of pain and suffering, but it doesn't automatically follow. So, in evaluating a reputation, ask what the reputation is for.

Generally, the longer an attorney has been practicing, the less significant is where he went to school and how well he did there. A high class ranking at a fine school is quite important if you're employing a new young lawyer. When he has been practicing for thirty years, what he has done more recently is probably more significant.

A publisher of a legal directory, which is a set of books listing virtually every practicing lawyer in the United States, is Martindale-Hubbell. Their directory is available in most libraries, and in virtually all law libraries. You can look up an attorney and find in all cases how old he is, when and where he went to college and to law school. In most cases, you can also find a "rating," which is an evaluation resulting from expressions of the other lawyers in the community. It's not necessarily reliable, but most lawyers would prefer an "A" rating to a "B," and so forth. Bar associations can also in some cases supply an inquirer with information with respect to specific attorneys, although you'll seldom hear negative comments there.

Recommendations of other clients are important, but should be taken with a grain of salt. Usually, one who has employed and used and paid for the services of an attorney, and had a satisfactory result from the encounter will speak highly of his counsel, if for no other reason than that he would like to think that he has chosen well. As with any profession, the purchaser of the services often is in no position to accurately evaluate the services he bought. Lawyer X handled a case for client A and won a judgment of $100,000. Client A thinks that X hung the moon, while in reality the case was worth $300,000 and X did a miserable job. Lawyer B, on the other hand, defended Y in a case where Y ended up with 90 days in jail. Y thinks that B is a jack-leg dog who ought to be disbarred, he handled the case so poorly, whereas, truth be known, B should have gone to prison for life. The way in which Y handled that case was sheer genius, and the videotape of the hearings is being used as a teaching tool all over the country. You never know.

Last, and most important, when you make a tentative choice or two, go ask for an interview. Talk to the attorney whose reputation you have heard about, and whose credentials you have checked out. See what the chemistry is; make a determination as to whether the two of you can work together as a team. Is he easy to talk with, or is he pompous and arrogant? Is he wishy-washy? forceful? vigorous? honorable? dependable? available? Does his manner seem to give you a basis for confidence? These are very personal measures, and the type of lawyer who was just right for your brother-in-law's cousin may not be the type of person you need.

Ask how the lawyer will charge for services, and what the probable range of fees will run. It's not likely that you can get a flat price quote for this nature of work, but a general range can be expressed with some comfort. It's OK to ask, and to expect an answer. You ask how much a pair of socks will cost before you buy, don't you?

Once you've made your choice, commence working together and be honest with yourself in deciding how it's going. If you feel you have to make a switch, you can always do so, but the later in the game that the switch comes, the harder and the more expensive it's going to be.

A FEW FINAL THOUGHTS

Well, I guess that this sorta' wraps up our conversation. We've been talking so long that I feel as if we're family. Anyway, whether or not, I've been impressed with the excitement that you're beginning to feel about that business of your own. I certainly hope that the excitement lasts, because there is some hard work ahead of you, some long days, and probably a few disappointments mixed in with all the thrills.

There will probably be some opportunities that come your way for some short-cuts. Generally, however, as you've learned in lots of other contexts, if it sounds too good to be true, it probably is. If the slow uphill way is the path most of the other folks have taken to get there, there is probably a good reason that they chose that route; maybe it's best for you too.

The other old cliche to throw in here is the observation that the people that you run into or step over while climbing up the ladder are the same ones you run into on the way down. And they won't have forgotten.

Even if you're working all by yourself, there are all sorts of folks available to offer you a helping hand, and many of them, you'll find, really have something to offer, and are happy to do so. That lawyer you hired can continue to act as a sounding board and confidante; your accountant and your banker will continue to be interested in your success and, probably, willing and able to advise and listen. Your chamber of commerce and other community organizations are filled with folks who may be able to give you a boost. Don't be afraid to try them.

Last and most important, keep that sense of purpose and confidence that you came in here with in the first place. A friend of mine used to have a sign on his desk that said "Now tell me some reasons why it CAN be done." That's a good sign.

Good luck.

Articles of Incorporation of Nice Little Company, Inc.

The undersigned, acting as an incorporator of a corporation under the provisions of Chapter 271B of the Kentucky Revised Statutes, adopts the following Articles of Incorporation for such corporation.

ARTICLE I.

The name of the corporation shall be:

NICE LITTLE COMPANY, INC.

ARTICLE II.

The corporation is authorized to issue 1,000 shares of its common capital stock, each of which shares shall be equal to all other shares in voting rights, distribution of dividend rights and liquidation rights.

ARTICLE III.

The corporation shall engage in any business activity in which corporations may lawfully engage in the Commonwealth of Kentucky.

ARTICLE IV.

The initial registered office of the corporation and the name of the initial registered agent in that office are:

George Nice
1234 Something Street
Somewhere, Kentucky 40909

ARTICLE V.

The mailing address of the corporation's principal office is:

1234 Something Street
Somewhere, Kentucky 40909

ARTICLE VI.

The name and mailing address of the incorporator are:

William Biglawyer
5678 Whereas Street
Somewhere, Kentucky 40901

ARTICLE VII.

The initial directors of the corporation are:

George Nice   Elizabeth Nice
1234 Something Street   1234 Something Street
Somewhere, Kentucky 40909   Somewhere, Kentucky 40909

ARTICLE VIII.

(1) Any person who was or is a party or is threatened to be made a party to any threatened, pending or completed action, suit, or proceeding, whether civil, criminal, administrative or investigative (other than by an action or in the right of the corporation), by reason of the fact that he is or was a director, officer, employee or agent of the corporation, or is or was serving at the request of the corporation as a director, officer, employee or agent of another corporation, partnership, joint venture, trust or other enterprise, shall be indemnified by this corporation against the expenses (including attorney's fees), judgments, fines and amounts paid in settlement actually and reasonably incurred by him in connection with such action, suit or proceeding, if he acted in good faith and in a manner in which he reasonably believed to be in or not opposed to the best interest of the corporation, and with respect to any criminal action or proceeding had no reasonable cause to believe his conduct was un-

lawful. The termination of any action, suit or proceeding by judgment, order, settlement, conviction, or upon a plea of nolo contendere or its equivalent, shall not, of itself, create a presumption that the person did not act in good faith and in a manner which he reasonably believed to be in or not opposed to the best interests of the corporation, and with respect to any criminal action or proceeding, had reasonable cause to believe that his conduct was unlawful.

(2) Any person who was or is a party, or is threatened to be made a party to any threatened, pending or completed action, suit by, or in the right of the corporation, to procure a judgment in its favor by reason of the fact that he is or was a director, employee, officer or agent of the corporation or is or was serving at the request of the corporation as a director, officer, or agent of another corporation, partnership, joint venture, trust or other enterprise, shall be indemnified by this corporation against the expenses (including attorney's fees) actually and reasonably incurred by him in connection with the defense or settlement of such action or suit if he acted in good faith and in a manner which he reasonably believed to be in or not opposed to the best interest of the corporation and except that no indemnification shall be made in respect of any claim, issue or matter as to which such person shall have been adjudged to be liable for negligence or misconduct in the performance of his duty to the corporation unless and only to the extent that the court in which such action or suit was brought shall determine upon application that, despite the adjudication of liability, but in view of all circumstances of the case, such person is fairly and reasonably entitled to indemnity for such expenses which the court shall deem proper.

IN TESTIMONY WHEREOF, witness the signature of the incorporator this _____ day of _____, 1997.

_____
WILLIAM BIGLAWYER

STATE OF KENTUCKY)
)
COUNTY OF SOMEONE)

I, a Notary Public in and for the State and County aforesaid, do hereby certify that the foregoing Articles of Incorporation of Nice Little Company, Inc. were this day produced before me in said State and County and were signed and acknowledged by William Biglawyer as the incorporator thereof, to be his act and deed.

Witness my hand this _____ day of _____, 1997.
My commission expires _____.

_____
NOTARY PUBLIC, STATE-AT-LARGE, KY

The foregoing instrument was prepared by William Biglawyer, 5678 Whereas Street, Somewhere, Kentucky 40901.

_____
WILLIAM BIGLAWYER

Bylaws of
Nice Little Company, Inc.

ARTICLE I. **OFFICES.**

Section 1. Principal Office. The principal office of the Company shall be at 1234 Something Street, in the City of Somewhere, Commonwealth of Kentucky, and its location may be changed from time to time by the Board of Directors.

Section 2. Other Offices. The Company may have offices at such places, within and without the State of Kentucky, as the Board of Directors may designate.

ARTICLE II. **CAPITAL STOCK.**

Section 1. Certificates of Stock. The stock of the Company shall be represented by certificates prepared or approved by the Board of Directors, signed by the president and secretary, sealed with the seal of the Company, consecutively numbered, and shall bear the date of their issue.

Section 2. Consideration for Issue. No shares shall be issued except for an equivalent in money paid or labor done, or property actually received and applied to the purposes for which the Company was formed, and neither labor nor property shall be received in payment for shares at a greater value than the market price at the time such labor was done or property delivered.

Section 3. Stock Certificate Book and Transfers. The certificates shall be issued from stock certificate books which shall contain in the margin or stub of each certificate the name and address of the stockholder, the number of shares, the date of issue or transfer, whether said shares are originally issued, or transferred from some other stockholder, and a receipt signed by the stockholder or his authorized agent. Stock may be transferred on the books of the Company only by the stockholder or his duly authorized attorney, and no new certificates shall be issued until the former certificates for the same number of shares shall have been surrendered and canceled, except as hereinafter provided. Canceled certificates shall bear the date of cancellation and shall be pasted in the stock certificate book opposite the memoranda of issue.

Section 4. Lost Certificates. The Board of Directors may make such rules and regulations, consistent with these Bylaws, as they shall deem proper, concerning the issue, transfer and registration of lost certificates of stock.

Section 5. Stock Book. The Company shall keep at its principal office a book to be known as the stock book, containing the names, alphabetically arranged, of all the stockholders, showing their places of residence, the number of shares of stock held by them respectively, and the time when they respectively became the owners thereof.

ARTICLE III.   STOCKHOLDERS.

Section 1. Definitions. The stockholders referred to in this article are the persons appearing as stockholders on the books of the Company who are entitled to vote at meetings of stockholders.

Section 2. Meetings; Mailing of Notices. The books of the Company shall contain the last known post office address of each shareholder of record, and all notices required to be mailed to the shareholder of record, or to any shareholder, shall be directed to him at such address.

Section 3. Annual Meeting: Time, Place and Purpose. The annual meeting of the stockholders shall be held at the principal office of the Company not later than 60 days following the close of the fiscal year, or at such other time and place as the Board of Directors may designate, for the purpose of electing directors, and for the transaction of such other business as may properly come before the meeting.

Section 4. Annual Meeting: Notice. Notice of the time, place and purposes of the annual meeting shall be delivered personally or mailed to each stockholder, not less than ten days before the meeting.

Section 5. Annual Meeting: Voting for Directors. At each election of directors the votes shall be cast by ballot, and the directors shall be chosen by a plurality of the votes at such election.

Section 6. Annual Meeting: Order of Business. A proper order of business at the annual meeting shall include the following:

1. Roll Call.
2. Proof of Notice of Meeting.
3. Reading and Disposal of Unapproved Minutes.
4. Reports of Offices and Committees.
5. Election of Directors.
6. Other Business.

Section 7. Special Meetings: Call. Special Meetings of the stockholders may be called at any time by the Board of Directors or upon the written request of any director, or of any shareholder or shareholders holding in the aggregate one-fifth of the voting powers of all shareholders.

Section 8. Special Meetings: Notice. Except when otherwise regulated by statute, notice of the time, place and purposes of each special meeting of the stockholders shall be delivered personally or mailed to each stockholder at least ten days before the meeting.

Section 9. Meetings: Voting and Proxies. At all meetings of stockholders, every stockholder shall be entitled to vote in person, or by proxy (appointed by instrument in writing subscribed by him or his duly authorized attorney) and shall be entitled to one vote for each share of stock standing in his name on the books of the Company, except in all elections for directors of the Company, each shareholder shall have the right to cast as many votes in the aggregate as he shall be entitled to vote under the Articles of Incorporation, multiplied by the number of directors to be elected by such election; and each stockholder may cast the whole number of votes for one candidate, or distribute such votes among two or more candidates. Upon demand of any stockholder the votes upon any question before the meeting shall be by ballot.

Section 10. Meetings: Quorum. At all meetings of the stockholders, for all purposes other than the election of directors, and except as otherwise provided by law, a majority of the voting stock of the Company must be represented at the meeting, in order to constitute a quorum.

Section 11. Organization of Meetings. The Chairman of the Company shall act as Chairman and the Secretary of the Company shall act as Secretary, at all meetings of the stockholders, unless otherwise determined by the stockholders present at the meeting.

Section 12. Adjournment of Meetings. In the absence of a quorum at the time and place fixed for any meeting of the stockholders, the meeting may be adjourned from time to time by a majority in interest of the stockholders present, without notice other than by announcement at the meeting.

Section 13. Waiver of Notices and of Meetings. Any notice required to be given under this article may be waived by the person entitled thereto. Whenever it is provided in these Bylaws that corporate action may be adopted at a meeting of the shareholders called for that purpose, such corporate action may be adopted without a meeting, unless otherwise provided by law, if all the shareholders who would be entitled to vote upon the action, if such meeting were held, shall consent in writing to such corporate action being taken.

Section 14. Shareholders' Action Without a Meeting. The shareholders shall be authorized to act without a formal meeting on any matter permitted by statute upon compliance with relevant requirements therefor.

ARTICLE IV.   DIRECTORS.

Section 1. General Powers. The property and affairs of the Company shall be managed and controlled by the Board of Directors.

Section 2. Number, Term of Office. The number of Directors shall be within the discretion of the stockholders. They shall be elected at the regular annual meeting of the stockholders for a term of one year and until their successors are elected and qualified, provided, however, that at any regular or special meeting, the shareholders may by majority vote declare the terms of office of all directors to be terminated immediately, and, using cumulative voting principles, elect a new board consisting of such number of directors as the shareholders may determine.

Section 3. Vacancies. Vacancies occurring on the Board shall be filled for the unexpired term by majority vote of the remaining directors; and if there shall be no director remaining, then by plurality vote of the stockholders present at a meeting called for that purpose by any stockholder, upon like notice and in like manner as provided for an annual election.

Section 4. Place of Meeting. The Board of Directors may hold their meetings, except the annual meeting, within or without the State, at such place or places as they may from time to time determine.

Section 5. Annual Meeting. Immediately after the annual meeting of the stockholders, the Board of Directors shall hold an annual meeting at the place at which the stockholders' meeting occurred, for the election of officers and the transaction of any other business.

Section 6. Regular Meeting. The Board of Directors may fix the times and places for the holding of its regular meetings. No notice of regular meetings shall be required, but directors not present when the regular meetings are so provided for, shall be duly notified of the time and place fixed therefor.

Section 7. Special Meetings: Call and Notice. Special meetings of the Board of Directors shall be held whenever called by direction of the President or of any director upon at least three days' notice in writing, given personally or by mail or telegram, which notice shall state the time, place and purpose of the meeting.

Section 8. Meetings held by Consent; Waiver of Notice. A meeting of the Board of Directors may be held at any time and place and without notice by unanimous consent of the directors or with the presence and participation of all the directors. Any notice required to be given under this article may be waived by the person entitled thereto.

Section 9. Quorum: Adjournment of Meetings. At any meeting of the Board of Directors, except when otherwise provided by law or these Bylaws, a majority of all the directors shall constitute a quorum, and the Board of Directors shall act by a majority of those present at a meeting at which a quorum is present; but in the absence of a quorum the meeting may be adjourned from time to time by a majority of those present, without notice other than by announcement at the meeting.

Section 10. Meetings: Chairman and Secretary. At all meetings of the Board of Directors, the President of the Company shall act as Chairman, and the Secretary of the Company as Secretary except that if either or both of them shall be absent, a chairman or secretary, or both, may be chosen at the meeting.

Section 11. Directors' Action without Meeting. The directors shall be authorized to act without a formal meeting on any matter permitted by the Kentucky Revised Statutes upon compliance with relevant requirements therefor, such as KRS 271B.8-210.

ARTICLE V.   OFFICERS.

Section 1. Executive Officers. The executive officers of the Company shall be a President and a Secretary who shall be elected by the Board of Directors.

Section 2. Other Officers. The Board of Directors may elect a general manager, one or more vice presidents, a treasurer, assistant treasurers and assistant secretaries, and such other officers as they shall deem necessary.

Section 3. Combining Offices. One person may hold more than one office.

Section 4. Terms of Office: Removal. All officers shall be elected or appointed for a term expiring at the next annual election, but they shall be subject to removal at the pleasure of the Board of Directors by affirmative vote of a majority of the whole Board and vacancies may be filled by the Board.

Section 5. Chairman of the Board. The Chairman of the Board may, but need not be, one of the other elected officers of the Company. The responsibility of the Chairman shall be to preside at meetings of the Board of Directors and the meetings of shareholders and to perform such other and additional duties of an executive nature as the Board of Directors shall prescribe.

Section 6. President. The President shall be the chief executive officer of the Company, and, subject to the control of the Board of Directors, shall have general charge of its business and supervision of its affairs. He shall keep the Board of Directors fully informed and freely consult with them in regard to the business of the Company, and make due reports to them and to the stockholders. In addition to the powers and duties elsewhere provided for him in these Bylaws, he shall, when duly authorized thereto, sign, acknowledge and deliver, all contracts, orders, deeds, liens, guarantees, licenses and other instruments of a special nature. Subject to the Board of Directors, he shall have such other powers and duties as are incident to his office and not inconsistent with these Bylaws, or as may at any time be assigned to him by the Board.

Unless otherwise ordered by the Board of Directors, the President shall have the full power and authority in behalf of the Company to attend, act and vote at any meetings of stockholders of any corporation in which the Company may hold stock, and at any such meetings shall possess and exercise any and all rights incident to the ownership of such stock, which the Company as owner might have possessed and exercised if present. The Board of Directors, from time to time, may confer like powers upon any other person or persons.

Section 7. Secretary. The Secretary shall cause to be entered in the minute book the minutes of all meetings of the stockholders and of the Board of Directors; shall have charge of the seal, stock record book of the Company, and all other books and papers pertaining to his office, and shall be responsible for the proper issuing, recording, transfer and cancellation of the certificates of stock, for the giving of all notices, and for the making of all statements and reports required of the Company or of the Secretary by law. He shall affix the corporate seal to the certificates of stock when duly signed, and affix such seal, attested by his signature, to all instruments duly authorized and requiring a seal. He shall perform such other duties as are incident to his office, and shall have such other powers and duties, in addition to those elsewhere provided for him in these Bylaws, as may at any time be assigned to him by the Board of Directors.

Section 8. Other Officers. The Board of Directors shall prescribe the title, powers and duties of any other officer of the Company.

Section 9. Salaries. The salary and other compensation of all officers shall be fixed by the Board of Directors.

ARTICLE VI.   FINANCE.

Section 1. Banking. All funds and money of the Company shall be banked, handled and disbursed, and all bills, notes, checks and like obligations, and endorsements for deposit or collection, shall be signed by such officers and other persons as the Board of Directors shall from time to time designate, who shall account therefor to the treasurer as and when he may require. All money, funds, bills, notes, checks and other negotiable instruments coming to the Company shall be collected and promptly deposited in the name of the Company in such depositories as the Board shall select.

Section 2. Dividends. The Board of Directors may declare and fix the amounts and times of payment of dividends from the surplus profits arising from the business of the Company.

Section 3. Fiscal Year. The fiscal year of the Company shall begin on the first day of January, unless otherwise provided by the Board of Directors.

ARTICLE VII.   SUNDRY PROVISIONS.

Section 1. Seal. The corporate seal of the Company shall consist of two concentric circles between which shall be the name of the Company.

Section 2. Amendments. The authority to make, amend and repeal bylaws of the Company is specifically vested in the Board of Directors, subject to the power of the shareholders to change or repeal such bylaws.

Winken, Blinken & Nod
Partnership Agreement

This is an agreement entered into at Somewhere, Kentucky as of January 1, 1997, by the persons named below for the purposes stated, who have agreed to engage in the business described below.

ARTICLE I
ORGANIZATION AND ADMINISTRATION

1.1 <u>Name.</u> The name of the firm shall be Winken, Blinken & Nod (the "firm").

1.2 <u>Purpose.</u> The firm is organized for the manufacture and sale of ice cream.

1.3 <u>Voting.</u> All firm decisions shall be made by vote of a majority of partners except where otherwise provided on a specific issue. A partner who is not present may vote by written proxy. Each partner has one vote.

1.4 <u>Financial Statements.</u> Monthly operating statements and annual profit and loss statements and balance sheets shall be prepared and distributed to the partners.

1.5 <u>Expense.</u> Expenses incurred by partners on behalf of the firm are subject to reimbursement by the firm, subject to policies established by the firm from time to time.

1.6 <u>Amendments.</u> This Partnership Agreement may be amended from time to time by the partners upon a vote of majority of the partners, except that sections requiring more than a simple majority for action shall likewise require such greater vote to be amended. Any such amendment must be in writing and signed by a number of partners at least equal to the number of partners required for adoption.

    1.7   Dissolution. The firm may be dissolved by agreement of majority of the partners in which event the assets shall be used first to pay debts, including partners' drawing accounts, then to repay partners' capital accounts, and then to be divided among the partners in accordance with their Partnership Ownership Interests set forth in Section 2.3 herein.

ARTICLE II
CAPITAL AND OWNERSHIP INTERESTS

    2.1   Capital Contributions. The opening capital of the firm shall consist of the contributions made by the partners as set forth in the initial balance sheet of the firm, as of January 1, 1997.

    2.2   Capital Accounts and Drawing Accounts. Each partner shall have a capital account and a drawing account. Each partner's share of profits or losses shall be credited or charged annually to his capital account, and any partner may withdraw his share of profits once a year in accordance with section 4.2(a). No interest shall be paid or charged on credit or debit balances in either the drawing account or the capital account, unless expressly authorized by the firm.

For the purpose of this Agreement, "profit" and "loss" shall mean those amounts credited or charged as profit or loss on the books of the firm and distributed to the partners' capital accounts in accordance with the standard accounting practices of the firm.

    2.3   Partnership Ownership Interests. The partners shall have equal ownership interests in the assets of the firm (the "Partnership Ownership Interests").

    2.4   Additional Capital Contributions or Loans to the Partnership. Upon decision of the partnership, by a majority of its members, each partner shall contribute equally additional capital or loan funds to the partnership.

    2.5   Restriction on Partnership Borrowing, Guarantees or Suretyship. Neither the partnership nor any partner nor any partners shall, without the written consent of a majority of the partners, borrow against the credit of the partnership or in the name of the partnership, or pledge or assign any of the partnership property as collateral for any debt, or commit the partnership to act as endorser, guarantor or surety for the obligation of any other person.

ARTICLE III
MEETINGS OF THE PARTNERS

3.1 <u>Meetings of Partners.</u> A meeting of the partners shall be held in the main office of the partnership upon call by the Management Committee or upon call by a majority of the partners. Notice of the meeting may be oral or written, the notice need not be given any period of time in advance of the meeting nor shall it be necessary to specify the purpose or purposes of the meeting. Notice of a meeting called by a majority of the partners will be deemed given if the calling majority of the partners attempt, in good faith, to give actual notice to all the partners. Notwithstanding the generality of the foregoing, a partnership meeting to consider admission or expulsion of one or more partners, or to consider amendment of this Agreement, may be held only upon forty-eight hours' notice, which notice shall specify the purpose of the meeting.

3.2 <u>Quorum.</u> The called meeting shall not be convened unless a quorum of the partners are present in person or by written proxy at the beginning of the meeting. A written proxy may be general, or may be limited to specific issues, and may, but need not, specify the vote to be registered. A quorum shall consist of a majority of all the partners. A quorum shall not be lost by reason of the departure from the meeting, once convened, by one or more partners.

A quorum being present at a duly called meeting, a majority of the votes cast will determine any issue to be decided by the partnership, except where a greater vote is expressly required by this agreement.

ARTICLE IV
DETERMINATION AND DISTRIBUTION OF INCOME

4.1 <u>Determination of Partnership Income.</u> As used herein, the term "Partnership Income" shall include such amount as is reported by the firm's regularly maintained account to the Internal Revenue Service of the United States.

4.2 <u>Allocation of Partnership Income.</u> Partnership Income shall be allocated among the partners as follows:

    (a)   Winken shall be allocated fifty percent; Blinken shall be allotted thirty-five percent; and Nod shall be allocated fifteen percent.

    (b)   Notwithstanding the foregoing provisions, the partners may, by unanimous action, reallocate the income among the partners for any year or part thereof if, in the view of all partners, adjustments to overall allocation are required to avoid an unfair impact upon one or more partners.

4.3 <u>Drawings.</u>

(a) Each partner shall be entitled to receive drawings from the firm, in cash, immediately following the 15th day and the last day of each month. Such drawings shall be in such aggregate amount as the partners shall determine to be available, divided on the same ratio as their income interest bear to each other.

ARTICLE V
MANAGEMENT

5.1 The day-to-day operation of the firm shall be conducted by a Management Committee, consisting of those partners elected by the partners on an annual basis, with the election occurring at the first partners' meeting in January of each year. Such committee shall have full authority to act for and on behalf of the firm with respect to employment and compensation of associates and support personnel, with respect to purchases and expenditures of a normal and ongoing nature, and with respect to acceptance of and compensation for employments, provided, however, that such committee shall report to the partners currently and regularly upon all actions, and provided further that any determination of the Management Committee is subject to review by, and to being overruled by, action of the partners at any regular or special meeting. Partners shall be notified before implementation on sensitive personnel matters, major expenditures, and other issues of substantial effect upon all partners.

ARTICLE VI
WITHDRAWAL, RETIREMENT, EXPULSION,
DISABILITY OR DEATH OF A PARTNER

6.1 <u>Termination of a Partner's Interest.</u> A partner's interest in the firm shall terminate upon any of the following occurrences:

(a) Voluntary withdrawal or retirement of the partner upon sixty (60) days' written notice to the other partners.

(b) Expulsion of the partner by unanimous vote of the other partners.

(c) Determination by unanimous vote of the other partners that the partner is permanently disabled, such determination to be made only after the disabled person has been unable to perform his professional responsibilities for a period of not less than six months.

(d) Death of the partner.

6.2 <u>Payments to Terminated Partner.</u> Upon the termination of a partner's interest in the firm, the firm shall pay to the partner or to the partner's successor in interest the following sums to the extent that they exceed the terminating partner's obligation to the firm:

(a) <u>Payment for Capital.</u> The amount of the terminated partner's capital account as of the date of termination, payable without interest within ninety (90) days after the last day of the month of the date of termination. This payment is intended to be for the terminated partner's interest in partnership property under Section 736(b)(1) of the Internal Revenue Code. In determining the amount of the capital account, fixed assets shall be valued as agreed upon by the terminated partner and the firm, or in the absence of such an agreement at appraised value as determined by two qualified appraisers, one selected and paid by the terminated partner or his or her estate and one selected and paid by the firm. If the two appraisers do not agree as to value, they shall select a third appraiser whose fee shall be shared equally and whose determination shall be binding.

(b) <u>Payment for Receivables and Work in Process.</u> Any terminating partner shall remain entitled to and shall continue to receive income due him pursuant to paragraph 4.2(a) and (b) of this agreement for a period of twelve months from and after termination, at the end of which term all such entitlements shall cease. Said sums shall be paid within thirty (30) days of receipt by the Partnership. Such entitlements shall be determined for all purposes as though the terminating partner were a continuing partner, except that they shall not be subject to the minimum requirements set forth in paragraph 4.2(d).

(c) <u>Payment for Current Year's Net Profits.</u> The terminating partner's share of any undistributed surplus in the Operating Account of the Partnership shall be determined as of the last day of the month in which the date of termination occurred.

(d) <u>Collection for Current Year's Net Losses.</u> The terminating partner, except where termination is by reason of death, shall pay to the Partnership his pro rata share of the net operating losses of the Partnership as of the last day of the month in which the date of termination occurred. All payments shall be made within thirty (30) days of the last day of the month in which the date of termination occurred, or twenty days following notice of the amount due, whichever shall later occur.

6.3 <u>Payment of Insurance Proceeds Upon Death of Partner.</u> Notwithstanding the provisions of paragraph 6.2 above and paragraph 6.4 below, if at the time of a partner's death, there is in existence a life insurance policy which pays a lump sum benefit to the partnership as a result of the partner's death, then in that event, the partnership shall pay 60% of the insurance proceeds received, or $150,000.00, whichever sum is greater, to a beneficiary named by the deceased partner, or if no beneficiary has been named, to the partner's surviving spouse, or if none, to the partner's surviving child or children, or if none, to the partner's estate. Said payment shall be considered full and final payment for said partner's interest in the partnership in lieu of the provisions of 6.2(a) above insofar as those provisions relate to payments as a result of death. Further, in the event such insurance is in existence, neither the estate of the deceased partner nor the aforementioned beneficiaries shall have any obligation for contributions toward partnership debts or net losses, and both the estate of the deceased partner and the aforementioned beneficiaries shall be indemnified by the partnership for said debts.

6.4   Optional Dissolution of the Firm. At the option of the other partners, by unanimous vote of said other partners, they may elect within sixty (60) days of the termination of a partner's interest to dissolve the firm in which case all partners (including the terminated partner or his estate) shall share in the liquidation proceeds, and the terminated partner or his estate shall not receive the payments set forth in paragraph 6.2 above, except that the beneficiary of a deceased partner shall receive the 60% insurance proceeds referred to in paragraph 6.3.

ARTICLE VII
TRAVEL, ENTERTAINMENT, AND
CERTAIN OTHER EXPENSES

7.1   Each partner of the Partnership is expected to incur certain expenses in connection with promoting the partnership business, dues, continuing education, and automobile and travel expenses. Each partner shall account to the Partnership for such expenses as of the last day of each year, and shall be reimbursed for the expenses by the Partnership via a credit to his or her partnership capital account or partnership drawing account. Said expenses shall be treated as a special allocation item of partnership expense and shall be borne by the partner incurring said expenses as a reduction of his share of the Partnership Income computed without regard to such special allocation items.

ARTICLE VIII
ADMISSION OF ADDITIONAL PARTNERS

8.1 <u>Additional Partners.</u> Additional partners may be admitted to the firm at any time, and from time to time, by the consent and agreement of and upon such terms and conditions as may be set by unanimous agreement of the then existing partners of the firm, provided, however, that any entering partner shall be required, as a condition of admission, to execute and agree to be bound by this Agreement.

8.2 <u>Miscellaneous.</u> This agreement shall be controlled by and interpreted under Kentucky law, and shall be binding upon the heirs, assignees and personal representatives of the parties hereto.

Signed this _____ day of _____, 199___, by the partners.

Mountain and Valley, Ltd.
Certificate of Limited Partnership

The undersigned, having this day formed a Limited Partnership under the provisions of the Kentucky Revised Uniform Limited Partnership Act, make and sign this certificate.

1.   The name of the partnership is:

Mountain and Valley, Ltd.

2.   The address of the office and the name and address of the agent for service of process required to maintained are:

Rebecca J. Partner
1234 Straight Street
Los Angeles, Kentucky 48888

3.   The name and business address of the sole General Partner is:

Large Real Estate Development, Inc.
1234 Straight Street
Los Angeles, Kentucky 48888

4.   The mailing address for the limited partnership is:

1234 Straight Street
Los Angeles, Kentucky 48888

5.   The latest date upon which the limited partnership is to dissolve is March 31, 2015.

6.   The rights and obligations of the General Partner and of all Limited Partners are as defined in the Limited Partnership Agreement entered into by the partners and as specified in the Kentucky Revised Limited Partnership Act.

To evidence their adoption of the foregoing certificate, the General Partner and the founding Limited Partnership have signed and sworn to this certificate on the date stated above.

GENERAL PARTNER:

By: _____
President

LIMITED PARTNERS

_____   _____

_____   _____

_____   _____

COMMONWEALTH OF KENTUCKY   )
)
COUNTY OF SOMEWHERE   )

The foregoing instrument was acknowledged before me by Rebecca J. Partner, President of Large Real Estate Development, Inc., a Kentucky corporation, on behalf of the corporation.

This _____ day of _____, 199____.

My commission expires: _____.

_____
Notary Public
State at Large, Kentucky

COMMONWEALTH OF KENTUCKY)

)

COUNTY OF SOMEWHERE)

The foregoing instrument was acknowledged before me by a limited partnership.

This _____ day of _____, 199____.

My commission expires: _____.

_____

Notary Public
State at Large, Kentucky

This instrument was prepared by William Biglaywer, 5678 Whereas Street, Somewhere, Kentucky 40909.

_____

William Biglaywer

Limited Partnership Agreement

THIS IS A LIMITED PARTNERSHIP AGREEMENT (the "Agreement") entered into by Large Real Estate Development, Inc. a Kentucky corporation, referred to hereinafter as "General Partner," and those persons executing this Agreement as Limited Partners, collectively referred to hereinafter as "Limited Partners."

NOW, THEREFORE, the parties hereto agree:

A. FORMATION OF LIMITED PARTNERSHIP

(1) <u>Uniform Limited Partnership Act.</u> The parties hereby form a limited partnership pursuant to the provisions of the Kentucky Revised Uniform Limited Partnership Act.

(2) <u>Name.</u> The name of the Partnership is Mountain & Valley, Ltd.

(3) <u>Place of Business.</u> The principal place of business of the Partnership shall be 1234 Straight Street, Los Angeles, Kentucky, until changed by the designation of the General Partner.

(4) <u>Certificate of Limited Partnership.</u> The partners shall, concurrently with the execution of this Agreement, sign and acknowledge a Certificate of Limited Partnership pursuant to KRS 362.415 and cause the same to be filed in the office of the Secretary of State of the Commonwealth of Kentucky.

(5) <u>Term.</u> The partnership shall commence as of the date of filing and recording the Certificate of Limited Partnership referred to above, and shall continue for a period ending on the earlier of:

(a) March 31, 2015;

(b) The date on which all real property owned by the Partnership or in which the Partnership has a beneficial interest, is sold or otherwise disposed of; or

(c) The date on which the Partnership is voluntarily dissolved by agreement of the partners or is dissolved by operation of law or judicial decree.

(6) <u>Purpose.</u> The business and purpose of this Partnership shall be to purchase, hold for investment, develop, and sell real property and the personal property used in conjunction therewith.

B. <u>DEFINITIONS</u>

The terms set forth below shall be defined as follows:

(1) <u>Acquisition Cost</u> means the sum of the price paid for a property by the Partnership plus all costs of improvements, including, without limitation, renovation, refurbishment and rehabilitation, if any, reasonably and properly allocable to the property, plus acquisition fees, and other prepaid expenses related to the property and its financing.

(2) <u>Acquisition Fees</u> means the total of all fees and commissions paid by any person to any person, including any sponsor in connection with the purchase or development of any property by the partnership whether designated as acquisition fee, development fee, nonrecurring management fee, or any fee of a similar nature, however designated, but not a development fee paid to one not affiliated with a sponsor, in connection with the actual development of a project after acquisition of the land by the Partnership.

(3) <u>Adjusted Capital Contribution</u> means the capital contribution of the Limited Partners and the General Partner reduced by all prior distributions of net proceeds made to the Limited Partners and the General Partner.

(4) <u>Affiliate</u> means (a) any person directly or indirectly controlling, controlled by or under common control with another person; (b) any person owning or controlling fifteen percent (15%) or more of the outstanding voting securities of such other person; (c) any officer, director, or partner of such person; (d) if such other person is an officer, director, or partner, any company for which such person acts in such capacity.

(5) <u>Appraised value</u> means value according to an appraisal made by an independent qualified appraiser.

(6) <u>Capital Contribution</u> means the total initial investment and contribution to the capital of the Partnership in cash by an investor for a Unit, or the contribution to capital by a General Partner without deduction of organization or other expenses.

(7) <u>Cash Available for Distribution</u> means the excess of the total cash revenues generated by the Partnership's properties and other investments less aggregate cash disbursements, including debt amortization and interest, taxes, operating expenditures, Partnership expenses, and amounts set aside for restoration or creation of reserves.

(8) <u>Development Fees</u> means fees for packaging a partnership property including, but not limited to, negotiating and approving plans and undertaking to assist in obtaining zoning and necessary variances and financing for the specific property, either initially or at a later date.

(9) <u>General Partner</u> means Large Real Estate Development, Inc., a Kentucky corporation.

(10) <u>Limited Partner</u> means a person who has purchased one or more Units under the terms set forth in this agreement.

(11) <u>Net Proceeds</u> means the cash proceeds from a sale or refinancing of a property remaining after retirement of mortgage debt and all expenses relating to the transaction.

(12) <u>Partnership Management Fee</u> means the fee payable to the General Partner in accordance with this Agreement.

(13) <u>Person</u> means any natural person, partnership, corporation, association, or other legal entity.

(14) <u>Property</u> means the tract of land more fully described in Exhibit A, which is attached to and incorporated by reference into this Agreement.

(15) <u>Purchase Price</u> means the sum of the price paid for a property by the Partnership plus all costs of improvements, including, without limitation, renovation, refurbishment, and rehabilitation, if any, reasonably and properly allocable to the property, but does not include acquisition fees, loan points, prepaid interest, or other prepaid expenses.

(16) <u>Unit</u> means an interest in the partnership representing a contribution to the capital of the Partnership by a General or Limited Partner, as set forth below.

C. **PARTNERSHIP UNITS AND CAPITAL**

(1) <u>Capital Contribution of Partners.</u> The capital shall be contributed by the Limited Partners and the General Partner.

(2) The General Partner shall contribute to the Partnership in return for which it shall receive nine Units.

(3) Limited Partners, each of whom is a signatory to this agreement, shall deliver to the Partnership cash in the sum of $_____ for each

Unit purchased, it being understood that such additional Limited Partners may not exceed ten in number at the time of formation of the Limited Partnership, and it being further understood that such Limited Partners shall own, in the aggregate, no more than thirty-three Units.

(4) Nonassessability of Units. The Units are non-assessable. Once a Unit has been paid for in full, the holder of the Unit has no obligation to make additional contributions to capital.

(5) Capital Accounts. A capital account shall be established for each Limited Partner and for the General Partner. Loans made by any Limited Partner or the General Partner shall not be considered contributions of capital. Neither the Limited Partners nor the General Partner shall be entitled to withdraw any part of his capital account or to receive any distributions except as specifically provided herein; in no event shall a Limited Partner or the General Partner have a right to receive property other than cash. No interest shall be paid on any capital invested in the Partnership.

(6) Liability of Limited Partner. Notwithstanding anything to the contrary in the foregoing, a Limited Partner shall not become liable for obligations of the Partnership in an amount in excess of his capital contribution.

D. MANAGEMENT

(1) Control in General Partner. Except as otherwise expressly stated in this Agreement, the General Partner shall have exclusive control over the business of the partnership, including the power to assign duties, to sign deeds, notes, deeds of trusts and contracts, and to assume direction of business operations. Without limiting the generality of the foregoing, such powers include the right to:

(a) Acquire, lease, and hold real property or interest therein at such price and upon such terms and conditions as he may deem proper, and to sell, exchange, convey, and refinance any or all of the partnership properties (subject to approval of the Limited Partners) in the event of the sale or exchange of all or substantially all of the assets of the Partnership.

(b) Reinvest net proceeds to (1) rehabilitate, renovate, or refurbish properties; (2) pay operating costs of properties if in the opinion of the General Partners it is necessary; and (3) establish reasonable contingency reserves.

(c) Borrow money on behalf of the Partnership and, as security therefor, to encumber the Partnership's properties or place title in the name of a nominee for the purpose of obtaining such financing, or for any other benefit to the Partnership.

(d) Prepay in whole or in part, refinance, increase, modify, or extend any obligation of the Partnership.

(e) Manage Partnership properties or employ and supervise a property manager.

(f) Employ from time to time at the expense of the Partnership persons required for the operation of Partnership business, including building management agents, other onsite personnel, insurance brokers, real estate brokers, and loan brokers, accountants, attorneys, and others on such terms and for such compensation as the General Partner determines to be reasonable. In this regard, the General Partner may, but shall not be obligated to, contract with persons, firms or entities who are, or who are affiliated with, one or more General or Limited Partners, so long as the terms of such arrangement are no less favorable to the Partnership than those generally available in the business community.

(g) Pay all organizational expenses incurred in the creation of the Partnership and all expenses incurred in connection with its operation.

(h) Assume the duties imposed on the General Partner by the Uniform Limited Partnership Act.

(2) <u>Limitations on General Partner's Authority.</u> The General Partner shall not have authority to:

(a) Do any act in contravention of this Agreement;

(b) Do any act which would make it impossible to carry on the ordinary business of the Partnership;

(c) Confess a judgment against the Partnership;

(d) Possess Partnership property or assign the rights of the Partnership in specific property for other than a Partnership purpose;

(e) Admit a person as a General Partner;

(f) Sell all or substantially all of the assets of the Partnership without the prior affirmative vote of Limited Partners owning a majority of the outstanding Units;

(g) Amend this Agreement without the prior affirmative vote of Limited Partners owning a majority of the outstanding Units;

(h) Dissolve the Partnership without the prior affirmative vote of Limited Partners owning a majority of the outstanding Units;

(i) Issue any additional Units beyond those described in this agreement, except with the written consent of the holders of eighty percent of the Units held by Limited Partners;

(j) Commingle or permit the commingling of the funds of the partnership with the funds of any other person;

(k) Invest the funds of the Partnership in limited partnership interests of other limited partnerships.

E. RIGHTS OF LIMITED PARTNERS

(1) No Limited Partner, as such, shall take part in the management of the business, transact any business for the Partnership, or have the power to sign for or bind the Partnership to any agreement or document.

(2) Notwithstanding the foregoing, the holders of two-thirds of the outstanding Units owned by Limited Partners may without the concurrence of the General Partner, vote to (a) dissolve the Partnership, (b) remove the General Partner and elect a new General Partner (see Section M), and (c) approve or disapprove the sale of all or substantially all of the assets of the Partnership. The holders of two-thirds of such Units shall have the power to amend this Agreement without the concurrence of the General Partner.

(3) The Limited Partners and their designated representatives shall have access to all books and records of the Partnership at all reasonable times. A list of the names and addresses of all Limited Partners shall be maintained as part of the records of the Partnership and shall be made available on request to any Limited Partner or his representative for the cost of reproduction.

F. INVESTMENT AND OPERATION POLICIES

(1) The Partnership capital shall be invested in the Property, or in shopping centers, apartments, office buildings, industrial properties, hotels, and other improvements located upon the Property.

(2) The Partnership shall not invest in excess of ten percent of its total capital contribution in junior mortgages and other similar obligations.

(3) It is contemplated that the sole activity of the Partnership will be the development and sale of those tracts of land comprising the Property. The Partnership may, however, elect to retain ownership of one or more of such tracts and to lease them to others, provided, however, that any lease for a term in excess of three years shall be entered into by the General Partner for the Partnership if and only if owners of not less than two-thirds of the total number of Units owned by Limited Partners shall have consented thereto, either by delivery of written consent to the Partnership or by affirmative vote at a meeting called by the General Partner, the notice for which specifies the terms of the lease to be considered.

(4) Investments of Partnership assets other than those related to the development of the Property shall be solely for the purpose of securing a

reasonable return on Partnership funds until needed to meet existing or reasonably foreseen Partnership expenditures or to satisfy other Partnership obligations or until the next distribution of earnings and proceeds to Partners.

G. GENERAL PARTNER'S LIABILITY AND ACTIVITY

(1) The General Partner (a) shall be held harmless and be indemnified by the Partnership for any liability suffered by them solely by virtue of acting as General Partner for the Partnership in connection with its activities; and (b) shall not be liable to the Partnership, nor to the Limited Partners, for any loss suffered by the partnership or the Limited Partners in connection with the Partnership's activities, provided that if such loss or liability arises out of any action or inaction of the General Partner, the General Partner must have determined, in good faith, that such course of conduct was in the best interests of the Partnership and, provided, further, that such indemnification or holding harmless shall only be recoverable out of the assets of the Partnership and not from the Limited Partners. The General Partner's entitlement to indemnity and relief from liability shall not apply, however, in the event of gross negligence or gross misconduct.

(2) Neither the General Partner nor any affiliate shall be bound to devote all of its business time to affairs of the Partnership, it being understood that they are and will continue to be engaged in other activities and in other employment, some of which may be in connection with business investments and other enterprises that may be in competition with the Partnership.

H. ACCOUNTING, RECORDS, REPORTS, MEETINGS

(1) Books and records of the Partnership shall be kept in accordance with generally accepted accounting procedures, and shall be available for inspection by any partner or his representative at all times during ordinary business hours, with copies thereof being made available in return for the reasonable cost of such copying.

(2) The General Partner will report periodically to all Limited Partners, in writing, with respect to the business of the Partnership. Interim reports will be rendered at least at quarterly intervals, and full reports will be supplied annually.

(3) A meeting of Partners may be held upon the call of the General Partner or upon the request of any three Limited Partners at such place and at such time as the party or parties requesting the meeting shall designate, for any purpose reasonably contemplated by the terms of this agreement or by the Kentucky Revised Uniform Limited Partnership Act.

I. ALLOCATIONS AND DISTRIBUTIONS

(1) <u>Allocations.</u> The profits, gains, and losses of the Partnership and each item of gain, loss, deduction, or credit entering into the computation thereof shall be determined for each fiscal year in accordance with the accounting methods followed for federal income tax purposes and otherwise in accordance with generally accepted accounting principles and procedures. Such profits, gains, and losses shall be allocated to each Limited Partner and the General Partner on an equal per Unit basis.

(2) <u>Cash Available for Distribution.</u> The Partnership shall make quarterly distributions of cash available for distribution, as such amount is determined by the General Partner, after establishment of such reserves as are required or are deemed prudent by the General Partner, *provided,* that no such distribution is contemplated during the first twelve months of operation of the Partnership. Forty percent of the cash available for distribution shall be paid to the General Partner as compensation for Partnership management and administration. The balance of cash available for distribution shall be allocated to each Limited Partner and the General Partner on an equal per Unit basis.

J. TRANSACTIONS BETWEEN GENERAL PARTNERS AND PARTNERSHIP

(1) <u>Reimbursement for Expenses.</u> The General Partner shall be reimbursed monthly by the Partnership for all expenses incurred in operating the Partnership and developing and selling properties of the Partnership. These expenses may include, but shall not be limited to, out-of-pocket expenditures for purchases, supplies, services, equipment lease or operation (including reasonable rental rates on equipment owned by the General Partner and used by or for the benefit of the Partnership), utilities, advertising, telephone, general office expenses, real estate commissions paid to others (but not to either Founding Limited Partner or his or their affiliate), rent, salaries and related perquisites and taxes, and, generally, all costs and expenses reasonably necessary and actually encountered. *Provided, however,* that the compensation of each Founding Limited Partner thus reimbursed as an expense deducted prior to determining profits and losses, and distributions set forth herein, shall not exceed the sum of Five Hundred dollars per week of full-time employment by the General Partner.

(2) <u>Management and Administration Fee.</u> In return for the General Partner's acting as manager of the Partnership's property or properties, it shall be paid compensation as set out above for all services rendered.

K. ASSIGNMENT OF INTEREST; SUBSTITUTED LIMITED PARTNER

(1) <u>General Partners.</u> The interests of the General Partner shall not be assignable in whole or in part, except when a substitution is made by vote of the Limited Partners.

L. DEATH OR INCOMPETENCY OF A LIMITED PARTNER

(1) <u>Effect on Partnership.</u> A Limited Partner's death or incompetency shall not cause a dissolution of the Partnership or entitle the Limited Partner or his estate to a return of capital.

(2) <u>Rights of Personal Representative.</u> On the death or incompetency of a Limited Partner, his personal representative shall have all the rights of a Limited Partner for the purpose of settling his estate, including the power of assignment.

M. RETIREMENT, REMOVAL, BANKRUPTCY, OR DISSOLUTION OF GENERAL PARTNER

(1) <u>Removal of General Partner.</u> An affirmative vote of the holders of two-thirds of the Units owned by all Limited Partners may remove General Partner. Written notice of such determination setting forth the effective date of such removal shall be served on the General Partner and shall terminate all of its rights and powers as a General Partner as of that date.

(2) <u>Dissolution of Partnership and Continuance of Partnership Business.</u> The retirement, removal, and adjudication of bankruptcy or dissolution of the General Partner (any of which events are referred to hereafter as the "terminating event") shall immediately destroy the agency relationship between the Limited Partners and the General Partner. A terminating event shall also dissolve the Partnership unless the business is continued by a General Partner elected by a vote of two-thirds of the Units held by the Limited Partners, who shall meet within 10 days of the terminating event and either:

(a) Elect to continue the business of the Partnership, provided a new General Partner is available and is so elected by such two-thirds vote of the Limited Partners, in which event a new certificate of limited partnership shall be recorded naming the new General Partner; or

(b) Elect to terminate and liquidate the Partnership under the provisions of this Agreement.

(3) <u>Payment to terminated General Partners</u>

(a) On the occurrence of a terminating event, if the business of the Partnership is continued, as aforesaid, the terminating General Partner shall be entitled to receive from the new General Partner or Partners as the case may be, the then-present value of their interest liquidation as determined by agreement of the terminated General Partner and the acquiring General Partner or Partners or, if they cannot agree, by arbitration in accordance with the then-current rules of the American Arbitration Association. The amount determined to be due together with any other sums due the Terminated General Partners shall be paid to them by promissory note bearing interest at the rate of ten percent per annum with the interest payable annually and the principal payable, if at all, from net proceeds which the terminated General Partners otherwise would have been entitled to receive pursuant to this Agreement. Any amounts received pursuant to this Agreement shall constitute complete and full discharge of all amounts to which the terminated General Partners are entitled hereunder.

(b) On the occurrence of a terminating event, the interest of the terminated General Partner evidenced by its capital contribution shall continue to be held by the terminated General Partner. (The remainder of the Partnership agreement consists of provisions relating to payments to creditors on dissolutions, required signatures on deeds and other documents, powers of attorney, and other miscellaneous items.)

N. DISTRIBUTION UPON DISSOLUTION OF LIMITED PARTNERSHIP

Upon the dissolution of the Limited Partnership, the General Partners, or such other person or persons acting on behalf of the Limited Partnership to accomplish the distribution, shall apply the assets of the Partnership in the following order:

(1) All assets of the Partnership shall be reduced or converted to cash in the most productive and most expeditious manner, as determined by the General Partner.

(2) All outstanding liabilities of the Partnership shall be paid in full from the assets of the Partnership.

(3) After establishment of a reasonable reserve for taxes, expenses of dissolution, and other reasonably foreseeable debts or liabilities, all remaining assets of the Partnership shall be distributed among the Limited and General Partners pro rata in the same proportions as distributions are then

being made under the provisions of paragraph I(3) above, provided, however, that in the event that any Limited Partner has not received the full amount to which he is entitled under the provisions of paragraph I(2) above, such distributions shall be made prior to distribution to any other partners.

O. TRANSFER OF LIMITED PARTNERSHIP INTEREST

(1) <u>Limitation Upon Transfer.</u> No Limited Partner may sell, assign, transfer, pledge, hypothecate, or otherwise dispose of or encumber his interest in the Partnership, except as is permitted in this section.

(2) By instrument of assignment, in form acceptable to the General Partner, a Limited Partner may transfer, assign, or give his interest in any one or more than one (but not fractional) units of Partnership Interest to his or her spouse, direct descendant, or spouse of direct descendant, or to a trust created for the benefit of any such person; provided, however, that any unit or units thus transferred shall remain subject to all the terms and provisions of this agreement as though the transferee were an original signatory hereto.

(3) In the event of the death of a Limited Partner, upon notice thereof to the General Partner, the unit or units held by such Limited Partner shall be deemed to be held by the personal representative of such decedent and, upon assignment and distribution of the estate of such decedent, such distributee shall be substituted as a new Limited Partner, provided, however, that such distribution may be in whole units only, and not fractional units, and provided, further, that such distribution may be made only to heirs at law, the surviving spouse, or direct descendants of the original Limited Partner, or to trusts created for their benefit under the will of the deceased Limited Partner. Any unit or units thus transferred shall continue to be subject to the provisions of this agreement as though the transferee or transferees were original parties hereto.

(4) In the event that any Limited Partner shall seek to transfer, sell, or otherwise dispose of his or her units of Limited Partnership, or any of them, in any manner than that set forth in the foregoing subparagraphs, and in the event the such Limited Partner shall have received a bona fide offer from an unrelated third party, he shall promptly communicate such offer, including price, terms and other relevant provisions, to the General Partner. The General Partner shall have a period of thirty days within which to elect to purchase the unit or units thus offered for sale by meeting the proposed terms of the transaction, or, if the General Partner so elects, to transfer and assign such right to purchase to any or all of the other Limited Partners. If such offer shall not have been accepted by the General Partner, or by a Limited Partner who is an assignee of the General Partner, within the described thir-

ty-day period after notice, the offering Limited Partner shall be permitted to transfer the described unit or units (in whole numbers only) to the proposed transferee upon the terms and conditions previously offered to the General Partner. Such permission shall remain open for a term of thirty days from and after the expiration of the original sixty day period, after which the right to transfer created hereunder shall cease. Notwithstanding the generality of the foregoing, no unit of Limited Partnership interest may be transferred under the provisions of this subparagraph at any time within one year from the date of this agreement, or at any time to any non-resident of the Commonwealth of Kentucky, without the written consent of the General Partner first obtained.

P. GENERAL PROVISIONS

(1) Conveyances. Any deed, bill of sale, mortgage, deed of trust, lease, contract of sale, or other commitment purporting to convey or encumber any interest of the Partnership in all or in any portion of any real or personal property at any time held in its name, shall be signed by General Partner on behalf of the Partnership, and no other signature shall be required.

(2) Any dispute or controversy arising in connection with this agreement, or in connection with the dissolution of the Partnership, or in connection with the respective rights and liabilities of the General and Limited Partners hereunder, shall be determined and settled by binding arbitration to be held in the City of Los Angeles, Kentucky, in accordance with the rules then obtaining to the American Arbitration Association. Any award rendered therein shall be final and binding on every Partner, and judgment may be entered thereon in the Jefferson Circuit Court, Los Angeles, Kentucky.

(3) Binding Effect. The provisions of this agreement shall be binding upon, and shall inure to the benefit of, the heirs, executors, administrators, successors, and assigns of each Partner.

(4) Entire Agreement. This instrument contains the entire understanding and agreement among the parties hereto respecting the subject matter hereof. There are no representations, agreements, arrangements, understandings, or undertakings, oral or written, between or among the parties hereto relating to the subject matter of this agreement not fully expressed herein.

(5) Applicable Law. This agreement shall be governed by and construed in accordance with the laws of the Commonwealth of Kentucky. Any matter not fully covered herein shall be governed by the provisions of the Revised Uniform Limited Partnership Act of the Commonwealth of Kentucky.

(6) <u>Subscription Agreement.</u> As a condition of becoming a Limited Partner, each person shall execute a subscription agreement in terms substantially identical to those contained on the exhibit attached hereto and entitled "Subscription Agreement."

To evidence their understanding of, and acceptance of all of the foregoing provisions, the parties have executed this agreement at Louisville, Kentucky, each on the date set forth opposite his signature below, it being understood that this agreement shall be effective upon all parties, and for all purposes, as of _____, 19___.

GENERAL PARTNER:

_____

By: _____
President

LIMITED PARTNERS:

_____

Print Name _____

Address _____

_____

Print Name _____

Address _____

_____

Print Name _____

Address _____

_____

Print Name _____

Address _____

Index